# AUBURN

# DAILY DEVOTIONS FOR DIE-HARD FANS

# TIGERS

# AUBURN

*Daily Devotions for Die-Hard Fans: Auburn Tigers*
© 2010 Ed McMinn

Library of Congress Cataloging-in-Publication Data
13 ISBN Digit ISBN: 978-0-9801749-8-4

Manufactured in the United States of America.

Go to http://www.die-hardfans.com for information about other titles in the series.

Cover and interior design by Slynn McMinn.

# AUBURN

Gibson, Daniel 46
Gibson, Upshaw 67
Gillespie, Gordie 67
Godby, Linda 14
Gosha, Willie 75
Goulbourne, Eva 31
Gran, Eddie 20
Green, A.C. 47
Gross, Gabe 26
Hall, Wayne 59
Harbin, Levorn 27
Harris, Bob 58
Harris, Henry 45
Harris, Red 46
Hawke, Brett 35
Heisman, John 13, 15, 32
Henley, Terry 33, 54
Hitchcock, Billy 49
Homan, Angela 7
Housel, David 19
Howard, Lindsey 7
Hudson, John 34
Hudson, Tim 49
Humphrey, Donnie 2
Hunt, Bobby 8
Hustell, Wilbur 16
Jackson, Bo 17, 18, 40, 58, 78
Jesse, Tim 5
Jett, Gardner 37
Johnson, LaKeisha 3
Jones, Carolyn 22, 65, 87
Jones, James Earl 20
Jordan, Evelyn 30
Jordan, Shug 6, 10, 17, 21, 23, 25, 30, 33, 37, 39, 42, 44, 50, 63, 64, 68, 79, 80, 84
Kahn, Roger 36
Killingsworth, Marco 51
Kiphart, Ridlon 66
Kolen, Mike 6
Langner, David 33, 37
Leard, Ben 69
Lemmon, Jack 6
Lemons, Abe 49
Levine, Tony 77
Lindsey, Danny 81
Lockwood, Frank 46
Lombardi, Vince 40, 50, 63
Lorendo, Mac 54
Lorino, Tommy 41

Mack, Connie 64
Majors, Johnny 80
Maravich, Pete 21, 82
Marsh, David 35, 43
McClurkin, Jim 64
McGraw, Tug 71
McHale, Kevin 52
Meagher, Jack 83, 86
Meeks, Bob 34
Merritt, Marianne 22
Michaels, Al 59
Miller, Shannon 10
Miska, Jason 59
Moore, Ashley 29
Moore, Jeff 53
Morris, Chris 53
Moulton, Slick 70
Newell, Kirk 46
Newkirk Sandra 57
Newman, Brock 35
Newton, Bill 33, 37
Nix, Lloyd 4, 41
Nix, Patrick 75, 89
Nix, Paul 82
Noll, Chuck 9
Ogletree, Craig 34
Oliver, Bill 26
Orr, Vickie 87
Owens, James 45
Owens, Jesse 79
Paige, Leroy 72
Payne, Marita 14
Person, Chuck 53
Petrie, George 1, 90
Petrie, Mary 29
Pyburn, Jim 17
Ramage, Diana 11
Rawson, Lamar 4
Reese, Eddie 85
Reif, Derek 49
Renfroe, Steve 76
Retton, Mary Lou 24
Reynolds, Walker 56, 73
Richardson, Tony 74
Riddle, David 7
Robinson, Brian 59, 75
Robinson, Eddie 81
Robinson, Robbie 46
Rockne, Knute 70
Ross, David 49
Royal, Darrell 41
Rupp, Adolph 38
Russell, Ann 79
Russell, Torrance "Bo"

16, 79
Ruth, Babe 43
Sanders, Frank 75, 89
Shirey, John 70
Shirling, Ed 67
Shore, Eric 66
Sidle, Jimmy 50
Simmons, Johnny 33
Simpson, Howard 50
Sinkwich, Frank 64
Slack, Reggie 34
Sloan, John 32
Smith, Bryant 18
Smith, Fred 59
Smith, Osmo 16
Smith, Sonny 53
Smith, Tre 20
Smith, Zeke 41
Spiller, C.J. 61
Spry, Ralph 31
Spurrier, Steve 75
Staubach, Roger 62
Stevens, Craig 52
Sullivan, Pat 5, 39, 40, 47, 63
Sutton, Ricky 74
Tate, Walter 74
Taylor, Courtney 81
Thomas, Frank 23
Tillman, Lawyer 5
Trason, Ann 34
Trevino, Lee 51
Tuberville, Tommy 9, 20, 27, 62, 69, 80
Twilley, Howard 22
Umbach, Swede 48
Von Wyl, Jim 74
Wallace, Cooper 81
Walls, Randy 33
Wanyoike, Catherine 7
Warren, C.C. 32
Weaver, Earl 75
Welker, Bill 84
White, Stan 42, 74, 89
Wilkinson, Bud 54
Will, Sarah 83
Wilson, Jerry 4
Woodall, Woody 50
Wooden, John 1
Wright, Alexander 34
Young, Charlton 65
Zatopek, Emil 39

198

# TIGERS

Plexico, Van. "The History of Jordan-Hare Stadium." http://www.plexico.net.sg/jordanhare/jh_history1.html.

Rice, Justin A. "Spiller Delivers Knockout Blow." *The State*. 2 Nov. 2008. http://docs.newsbank.com/s/InfoWeb/aggdocs/NewsBank/12434A3FE4C4F2D8.

Robertson, Ryan. "Rowdy Gaines Shows He Never Gives Up." *The Auburn Plainsman*. 27 June 2007. http://www.theplainsman.com/node/2711.

Segrest, Doug. "Right Place, Right Time as Stevens Ices Game with Pick He Saw Coming." *The Birmingham News*, 20 Sept. 2009. 6B.

Scott, Richard. *An Inside Look at a Perfect Season: Tales from the Auburn 2004 Championship Season*. Champaign, IL: Sports Publishing, L.L.C., 2005.

Warner, Chris, ed. *SEC Sports Quotes*. Baton Rouge: CEW Enterprises, 2002.

Yi, Yun Mi. "Center Gives Opponents Payne." *The Auburn Plainsman*. 27 Jan 2005. http://www.cstv.com/sports/w-baskbl/uwire/012705abn.html.

Zenor, John. "Auburn Perfect, But Frustrated." 6 Jan. 2005. http://www.amarillo.com/stories/010605/col_972252.shtml.

# INDEX
(LAST NAME, DEVOTION DAY NUMBER)

Alvis, Ken 59
Ashe, Arthur 11, 28
Atkins, Billy 4
Atkins, George 4, 84
Bailey, Thomas 75
Baird, Hal 49
Baker, Tim 23
Bannister, Sir Roger 31
Barkley, Charles 31, 38, 60
Barnier, Romain 35
Barron, Red 70
Beard, Jeff 21, 86
Beasley, Terry 40, 47, 63
Beck, Dave 33
Beckwith, Bill 82
Beckwith, Joe 82
Bee, Clair 15
Berra, Yogi 8, 32, 53, 86
Bidez, P.R. "Bedie" 71
Binder, Adrienne 61
Bolton, Mae Ola 87
Bolton, Ruthie 87
Bolton, Scott 5
Bonner, Pete 32
Bostic, James 89
Bowden, Bobby 33, 74, 78, 89
Bowden, Terry 12, 26, 35, 42, 89
Bowman, Scotty 69

Bradberry, Buck 84
Bryant, Bear 37, 54
Burger, Jeff 5
Burks, Kenny 25
Campbell, Jason 81
Campbell, Randy 58
Canzoneri, Fagan 64
Carr, Greg 2
Casey, Herbert 74
Childress, Joe 17
Chizik, Gene 52
Ciampi, Joe 3, 22, 87
Ciarla, Aaron 35
Clark, Wallace 47
Costellos, Vic 64
Craig, Dameyune 88
Crain, Kurt 2
D'Agostino, Frank 17
D'Amato, Cus 46
Danley, Stacy 34, 74
Davalos, Rudy 45
Davis, Kyle 51
Davis, Stephen 75
de Vivie, Paul 58
Del Greco, Al 58, 78
Denniston, Dave 35
Dentmon, Justin 87
Diaz, Matt 49
Donahue, Bill 67
Donahue, Mike 10, 13, 32, 56, 67, 70, 71, 73

Dooley, Vince 3
Dragoin, Sonny 48
Dunn, Casey 49
Dunn, Don 80
Duva, Lou 27
Dye, Pat 2, 5, 19, 34, 62, 73, 78
Eaves, Joel 16, 38
Eddings, Liston 30
Ellis, Cliff 18
Erving, Julius 55
Esiason, Boomer 78
Evans, Kim 11
Farina, Laura 3
Fibbe, Jimmy 38
Ford, Frank 53
Fox, Chris 7
Frederickson, Tucker 8
Freeman, Bobby 17
Fullan, Thomas 71
Fuller, Andy 75
Fullwood, Brent 5
Fyffe, Jim 29
Gaines, Rowdy 72
Gainous, Trey 5
Gaither, Jake 16
Gargis, Phil 25
Garvey, Steve 48
Gibson, Charles 13

197

# TIGERS

*To Ted Heath,*
*a real Tiger*
*for God*

Where crouching tigers wait their hapless prey . . .
Sweet Auburn, loveliest village of the plain.
-- Oliver Goldsmith "The Deserted Village"

# IN THE BEGINNING

### Read Genesis 1, 2:1-3.

*"God saw all that he had made, and it was very good" (v. 1:31).*

In the beginning was a wilderness.

Settlers began building a village in east Alabama in 1836 and began to search for a name for their new community. One of the villagers returned to Georgia on a business trip where he met and fell in love with Lizzie Taylor of Jones County. He regaled her with tales of his town in Alabama, including the settlers' search for a name.

Fifteen-year-old Miss Lizzie had recently read Oliver Goldsmith's famous poem "The Deserted Village." She told the man who was to be her husband, "Oh, name it Auburn, sweet Auburn, loveliest village of the plain." And so she unknowingly named the place that was to be her home.

In the beginning was a village without a college. In 1857, the Alabama Conference of the Methodist Church founded East Alabama Male College. In 1872, it became the Agricultural and Mechanical College of Alabama. In 1899, the school became the Alabama Polytechnic Institute. In 1960, the name was officially changed to Auburn University.

In the beginning was baseball, which was about all the athletics the school had early on. While Auburn professor George Petrie was on a leave of absence to study for his doctorate at Johns

Hopkins in Baltimore, he made a trip to North Carolina and saw football played for the first time. He liked what he saw, and when he returned to Auburn in 1891, Petrie brought his enthusiasm for the new game with him. He offered to show the students how football was played and became the self-appointed coach without salary. Practices began and the team challenged Georgia. Within six weeks after the first team had been organized, Auburn beat Georgia 10-0 in Atlanta on Feb. 20, 1892.

Beginnings are important, but what we make of them is even more important. Consider, for example, how far the Auburn football program has come since that first game in 1892. Every morning, you get a gift from God: a new beginning. God hands to you as an expression of divine love a new day full of promise and the chance to right the wrongs in your life. You can use the day to pay a debt, start a new relationship, replace a burned-out light bulb, tell your family you love them, chase a dream, solve a nagging problem . . . or not.

God simply provides the gift. How you use it is up to you. People often talk wistfully about starting over or making a new beginning. God gives you the chance with the dawning of every new day. You have the chance today to make things right – and that includes your relationship with God.

*The most important key to achieving great success is to decide upon your goal and launch, get started, take action, move.*
*-- John Wooden*

**Every day is not just a dawn; it is a precious**
**chance to start over or begin anew.**

# GOD'S WORKFORCE

**Read Matthew 9:35-38.**

*"Then he said to his disciples, 'The harvest is plentiful but the workers are few. Ask the Lord of the harvest, therefore, to send out workers into his harvest field'" (vv. 37-38).*

**P**at Dye "hit town with fire in his gut." He threw two players out of the first team meeting he ever had with his Auburn football team in January of 1981. Things only got tougher after that.

Defensive tackle Donnie Humphrey, a member of Auburn's Team of the Century, said the first spring training under Dye was "the hardest thing I've ever been through. . . . There weren't many limits on what they could do to us." Humphrey said, "We started out that spring with something like 115-120 players and ended up with 75-80. They ran a lot of players off. If you weren't willing to put forth the effort, [the coaches] didn't want you around."

According to Humphrey, the Tigers "seldom practiced more than about an hour and a half" before Dye arrived. That changed drastically. "When Coach Dye got there, I think we went every day for about three or four weeks from 3:30-7:30." Humphrey said that by the time the players got to the 1981 season, they thought they could survive anything.

Work, work, and more work – that was the foundation of Dye's coaching approach. The coach "built a powerhouse on his beliefs of hard work and physical play. Dye believes football is a test of

will, of endurance, of willingness to sacrifice." "We worked so hard," Kurt Crain, an all-American linebacker under Dye said of those early days. "We thought we worked harder than anybody else."

Work worked at Auburn; the Dye years were among Auburn's greatest: a 99-39-4 record that included four SEC championships, four 10-win seasons, and – perhaps most importantly of all – a four-game winning streak against Alabama.

Do you embrace hard work or try to avoid it? No matter how hard you may try, you really can't escape hard work. Funny thing about all these labor-saving devices like cell phones and laptop computers: You're working longer and harder than ever.

For many of us, our work defines us perhaps more than any other aspect of our lives. But there's a workforce you're a part of that doesn't show up in any Labor Department statistics or any IRS records.

You're part of God's staff; God has a specific job that only you can do for him. It's often referred to as a "calling," but it amounts to your serving God where there is a need in the way that best suits your God-given abilities and talents

You should stand ready to work for God all the time, 24-7. Those are awful hours, but the benefits are out of this world.

*We weren't sure of anything when Coach Dye came in. But we did know that we were going to have to work.*
— *All-American Greg Carr*

**God calls you to work for him using the talents and gifts he gave you; whether you're a worker or a malingerer is up to you.**

# MAKEOVER ARTIST

**Read 2 Corinthians 5:11-21.**

*"If anyone is in Christ, he is a new creation; the old has gone, the new has come!" (v. 17)*

**O**kay, what'll you be at Auburn: a basketball player or a volleyball player? You can't be both because the seasons coincide. Well, LaKeisha Johnson managed to play both.

She was first and foremost a basketball player for the Tigers. She lettered four years and as a junior was the only player to start all 29 games in the 2001-02 season.

But volleyball was frequently on her mind. As a freshman she had spoken to head basketball coach Joe Ciampi about playing volleyball too. That's when she found out the volleyball season overlapped the basketball season.

Even if she could get in some volleyball games, such double duty only increased the danger of getting injured — too much risk for a player on scholarship valuable to the higher profile basketball team.

So Johnson contented herself with roundball. Until she completed her four years of basketball eligibility and was a fifth-year senior at Auburn in 2003 waiting for graduate school after majoring in psychology and minoring in business. Could she play volleyball now?

She approached volleyball coach Laura Farina, who was eager to take advantage of Johnson's skills and competitive instincts

honed by four years of SEC basketball. "I had certainly heard a lot of good things about her," Farina said. Together, they made it happen.

"I see this as a very positive thing," Johnson said, "because I played both sports all my life until college." LaKeisha Johnson the basketball player was made over into LaKeisha Johnson the outside hitter.

Ever considered a makeover? TV shows have shown us how changes in clothes, hair, and makeup and some weight loss can radically alter the way a person looks.

But these changes are only skin deep. Even with a makeover, the real you — the person inside — remains unchanged. How can you make over that part of you?

By giving your heart and soul to Jesus -- just as you give up your hair to the makeover stylist. You won't look any different; you won't dance any better; you won't suddenly start talking smarter.

The change is all on the inside where you are brand new because the model for everything you think and feel is now Jesus. He is the one you care about pleasing. Made over by Jesus, you realize that gaining his good opinion — not the world's — is all that really matters. And he isn't interested in how you look but how you act.

*Don't think that the way you are today is the way you'll always be.*
*-- Vince Dooley*

**Jesus is the ultimate makeover artist; he can make you over without changing the way you look.**

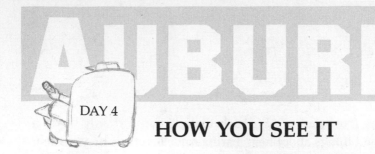

# HOW YOU SEE IT

**Read John 20:11-18.**

*"Mary stood outside the tomb crying" (v. 11).*

T he weather was awful.

Sept. 28, 1957, was miserably wet and rainy in Knoxville when the Tigers began their football season against Tennessee. Some 42,000 soaked fans shivered under raincoats and umbrellas, most of them Big Orange followers who showed up expecting to watch their team win easily. After all, the Vols were the preseason pick to win the SEC and were ranked in the top 10; Auburn wasn't ranked in the top 20.

In the second quarter, though, Jerry Wilson blocked a UT punt to set the Tigers up at their own 43, and they drove 57 yards for a touchdown in the mud. The big play came on third and six at the Tennessee ten when quarterback Lloyd Nix managed a "ground-skinner pitchout" just as he was clobbered. Halfback Lamar Rawson picked up the grounder and made the first down. Fullback Billy Atkins scored from the one on third down and then kicked the extra point. That 7-0 score held up, and Auburn had begun its run to the national championship.

So the miserable weather dampened everybody's spirits, right? It depends.

Sportswriter Benny Marshall said of the post-game atmosphere, the day "was cold and clammy and uncomfortable. A miserable sort of September Saturday. . . . Gray day, somber day, unhappy

day for Tennesseans. For Auburn it came out something altogether different. The sun was shining and birds must have been singing and all of that. Great day, wonderful day."

The day was wet and miserable on the Tennessee sideline, but only a few yards away, the weather could not have been better for the Tigers and their fans. In fact, "never had such a celebration broke[n] out on an Auburn sideline." It was all a matter of perspective.

Your perspective goes a long way toward determining whether you slink through life amid despair, anger, and hopelessness or stride boldly through life with joy and hope. Mary is a good example. On that first Easter morning, she stood by Jesus' tomb crying, her heart broken, because she still viewed everything through the perspective of Jesus' death. But how her attitude, her heart, and her life changed when she saw the morning through the perspective of Jesus' resurrection.

So it is with life and death for all of us. You can't avoid death, but you can determine how you perceive it. Is it fearful, dark, fraught with peril and uncertainty? Or is it a simple little passageway to glory, the light, and loved ones, an elevator ride to paradise?

It's a matter of perspective that depends totally on whether or not you're standing by Jesus' side when it arrives.

*Nobody knows how hard these boys have worked. There's no doubt in my mind. They're going to win it.*
*— Auburn assistant Coach George Atkins before the '57 UT game*

**Whether death is your worst enemy or**
**a solicitous chauffeur is a matter of perspective.**

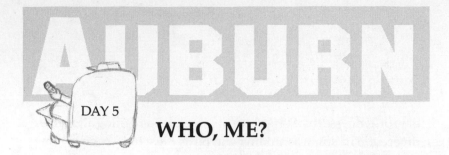
DAY 5

# WHO, ME?

### Read Judges 6:11-23.

*"'But Lord,' Gideon asked, 'how can I save Israel? My clan is the weakest in Manasseh, and I am the least in my family'" (v. 15).*

One of the most memorable moments in the history of Auburn football was a botched play.

Wide receiver Lawyer Tillman reversed himself into Auburn immortality by scoring from the seven with only 32 seconds left to whip Alabama 21-17 at Legion Field on Nov. 29, 1986. But Tillman wasn't even supposed to be a part of the breathtaking finish.

All-American fullback Brent Fullwood galloped for a 26-yard touchdown on the first play of the fourth quarter to cut Alabama's lead to 17-14. After converting a fourth down on a pass from Jeff Burger to wideout Trey Gainous, the Tigers drove to the Crimson Tide seven as time was running out.

The noise was so intense when the Tigers huddled that Tillman couldn't hear quarterback Burger's play call. Then when they broke for the line, he saw Coach Pat Dye "jumping up and down on the sideline, signaling timeout." Puzzled, Tillman looked over to his quarterback, who understood the receiver's problem. Burger simply shouted the play out to Tillman -- eighteen reverse left -- "knowing Alabama's defense couldn't hear him because he couldn't hear himself."

When he heard the play, Tillman knew why Dye was so frantic.

He didn't run the reverses; his backup, Scott Bolton, did. Tillman wasn't supposed to be in the game! So he joined Dye's pantomime, but Burger was already taking the snap. Thankfully for Auburn history and lore, nobody wearing stripes noticed Tillman's or Dye's hand signals.

Burger pitched to tailback Tim Jesse, who swept right. Tillman dutifully ran the play, took the pitch from Jesse going the other way, and covered the seven yards into Tiger immortality.

Who, me? You probably know exactly how Lawyer Tillman felt.

How about that time the teacher called on you when you hadn't done a lick of homework? Or the night the hypnotist pulled you out of a room full of folks to be his guinea pig? You know the look and the sinking feeling in your stomach. You've had it when you were suddenly singled out and found yourself in a situation you neither sought nor were prepared for.

You may feel as Gideon did about being called to serve God in some way, quailing at the very notion of being audacious enough to teach Sunday school, lead a small group study, or coordinate a high school prayer club. After all, who's worthy enough to do anything like that?

The truth is that nobody is – but that doesn't seem to matter to God. And it's his opinion, not yours, that counts.

*This is the biggest surprise I've ever had.*
*-- Pat Sullivan on the Heisman Trophy*

**You're right in that no one is worthy to serve God,**
**but the problem is that doesn't matter to God.**

# CHANCE MEETING

### Read Luke 24:13-35.

*"That same day two of them were going to a village. . . .*
*They were talking with each other about everything that*
*had happened. . . . Jesus himself came up and walked*
*along with them" (vv. 13-15).*

**M**uch about Captain Crunch's experience at Auburn was memorable, but what he remembered as the highlight were two encounters.

For Auburn football fans, Captain Crunch isn't a cereal; he's Mike Kolen, one of the greatest of Tiger linebackers. Kolen played from 1967-69 with such success that each spring the team's leading tackler from the season before is presented the Mike Kolen Award.

Playing for Coach Shug Jordan, Kolen was twice All-SEC after moving into a starting position his sophomore year. His senior season the Birmingham Quarterback Club named him the SEC's Most Valuable Player. The most unforgettable game of that 8-3 season in 1969 was a 49-26 blasting of Alabama. He went on to be a part of the incredible undefeated season the 1972 Miami Dolphins put together, the only one in pro football history.

Kolen's years at Auburn remain an integral part of his life, and his memories of the time spent there are fond ones. But his life was changed most not by what he accomplished while he was at Auburn, but rather by two persons he met there. Kolen has

said that he met the two most important people of his life at Auburn: "I became a Christian my freshman year at AU, so I met my saviour the latter part of my freshman year, and I met my wife my sophomore year."

A pair of on-campus meetings changed Mike Kolen's life forever.

Maybe you met your spouse on a blind date or in Kroger's frozen food section. Perhaps a conversation in an elevator or over lunch led to a job offer.

Chance meetings often shape our lives. Some meetings, however, are too important to be left to what seem like the whims of life. If your child is sick, you don't wait until you happen to bump into a physician at Starbuck's to seek help.

So it is with Jesus. Too much is at stake to leave a meeting with him to chance. Instead, you intentionally seek him at church, in the pages of your Bible, on your knees in prayer, or through a conversation with a friend or neighbor. How you conduct the search doesn't matter; what matters is that you find him.

Once you've met him, you should then intentionally cultivate the acquaintance until it is a deep, abiding, life-shaping and life-changing friendship.

*If you think it's hard to meet new people, try picking up the wrong golf ball.*

*-- Jack Lemmon*

**A meeting with Jesus should not be
one of life's chance encounters,
but instead should be sought out.**

# RAIN CHECK

**Read Genesis 9:8-17.**

*"I establish my covenant with you: Never again will all life be cut off by the waters of a flood; never again will there be a flood to destroy the earth" (v. 11).*

The ducks loved it -- and so did the Auburn cross-country teams.

"It" was the rain, which came down in good measure in Auburn on Friday, Oct. 10, 2003. Such a downpour usually puts a damper on outdoor athletic events -- everything from baseball and softball to track. Not cross country, though.

Even so, the performance has got to suffer, right? Well . . . ? Head coach Chris Fox said the Auburn squads ran "the best race we have run in a long time."

The men's team raced against 28 other teams in an 8K-run and won it, edging Georgia Tech and Tennessee and slogging past LSU, Mississippi State, and Vanderbilt among others.

The Auburn women competed against 31 other teams and placed third, trailing only Mississippi State and Indiana. Sophomore Angela Homan placed third, and senior Catherine Wanyoike splashed her way to fifth place.

Surely the Auburn runners were oppressed and depressed about having to run in such downright beastly conditions!

"It was fun," declared junior David Riddle. "For runners, it doesn't really matter. It is what cross country is all about."

# TIGERS

Fox explained that the weather -- good, bad, or indifferent -- isn't really a factor for his teams. "You stay in your routine, and you just show up for the race," the coach said.

The notion that sloshing around in the rain is a quite wonderful way to spend an afternoon was apparently shared by the Spikettes, the teams' hostess organization. They braved the rain and the mud to cheer their favorite athletes home.

The kids are on go for their picnic. Your golf game is set. You have ribeyes and smoked sausage ready for the grill when the gang comes over tonight. And then it rains.

Sometimes you can slog on through a downpour as the Auburn cross-country teams did. Often, however, the rain simply washes away your carefully laid plans, and you can't do anything about it.

Rain falls when and where it wants to without checking with you. It answers only to God, the one who controls the heavens from which it comes, the ground on which it falls, and everything in between -- territory that should include you.

Though God has absolute dominance over the rain, he will take control of your life only if you let him. In daily seeking his will for your life, you discover that you can live so as to be walking in the sunshine even when it's raining.

*It takes a special person to be out here in the rain.*
*-- Spikette President Lindsey Howard*

**Into each life some rain must fall,**
**but you can live in the glorious light of God's love**
**even during a downpour.**

# BAGGAGE CHECK

**Read Luke 5:17-26.**

*"Who can forgive sins but God alone?" (v. 21b)*

It was not the kind of impression that Tucker Frederickson the recruit wanted to make on the Auburn coaches.

Frederickson is in the minds of many the greatest football player in Auburn history. He has been called "a man before his time" in his combination of "size, speed, power and finesse. In 1963 and 1964, he was the best running back, the best blocking back and the best defensive back in the Southeastern Conference."

When the fans selected the Team of the Century in 1992, he got the most votes. He was All-America as a safety in 1964 and won the Jacobs Trophy as the South's best blocker. The New York Giants made him the first player chosen in the NFL draft after the 1964 season. He is a member of both the Alabama Sports and the College Football halls of fame.

But all that was ahead of him when Frederickson arrived in Auburn from Hollywood, Fla., as a recruit in the winter of 1961. "I was a kid that went up there scared to death," he recalled. He had flown into Montgomery from Florida for the trip and was taken to Sewell Hall to unpack for the weekend. When he opened his suitcase, its entire contents rolled out onto the carpet: three full bottles of Jack Daniels whiskey.

Quarterback Bobby Hunt smiled, whistled appreciatively, and then said to the assistant coach with them, "Now this is the kind

of guy we've been needing to recruit all along."

The suitcase, of course, wasn't Frederickson's; he had picked up the wrong bag at the airport. Still, he thought for a moment his chances at playing football for Auburn were over. "I figured they'd tell me to go home right then," he recalled.

No chance. Instead, the trip convinced Frederickson that Auburn was the ideal place for him even if he did have a rather unusual problem with his luggage.

The key to successful traveling is taking along only what we need. This applies to our journey through life too, but often we lug along excess baggage: the recriminations we carry from the mistakes we've made, the regrets from the love we failed to give, the memories of our failures. We allow our past to poison our present and darken our future.

Wouldn't it be great if you could just dump all that baggage on the equivalent of an emotional and mental porter, somebody with shoulders broad enough to take the whole load upon himself and set you free from its crushing and oppressive burden? Well, there is somebody, one for whom forgiveness is such a basic part of his nature that he sent his son to us to arrange it. That somebody is God. He'll take it all – every bit of it -- if you only have faith and trust enough to hand it over to him.

*Why buy good luggage? You only use it when you travel.*
—*Yogi Berra*

**One of the most heartbreaking mistakes
many people make is believing that the things
they've done are too awful for God to forgive.**

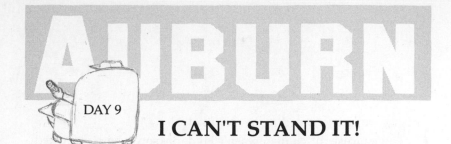

# I CAN'T STAND IT!

**Read Exodus 32:1-20.**

*"[Moses'] anger burned and he threw the tablets out of his hands, breaking them to pieces at the foot of the mountain" (v. 19).*

**H**ow can the greatest season in the history of Auburn football be frustrating?

In 2004, for the first time in their storied history, the Tigers won 13 games in a season. Their march to perfection and their first SEC title in 15 years included a thrilling 10-9 win over the defending national-champion LSU Tigers. Other than that, they waltzed through the SEC as though it were the WAC, whipping Tennessee 38-28 in Atlanta for the title. They capped the perfect season with a 16-13 win over Virginia Tech in the Sugar Bowl.

So how in the world could that be frustrating?

They wound up No. 2 in the nation without having a shot at the national championship many felt they deserved. Auburn was called "the third wheel in the Bowl Championship Series" with Southern California slaughtering Oklahoma 55-19 in the Orange Bowl for the title.

"I was disappointed that the type of team we had, as balanced as we were, we didn't get a chance to play in that game," Coach Tommy Tuberville said. He conceded USC was the best team on the field in Miami, but he refused to accept the notion that the Orange Bowl was the national championship game, saying

simply, "I beg to differ."

Auburn was hurt by its preseason No. 17 ranking, which made it virtually impossible to move into one of the top two spots even though, as Tuberville said, "You can't do any better." Under the BCS system, the Tigers could only play the frustrating hand they were dealt.

The traffic light catches you when you're running late for work or your doctor's appointment. The bureaucrat gives you red tape when you want help. Your child refuses to take homework seriously. Makes your blood boil, doesn't it?

Frustration is part of God's testing ground that is life even if much of what frustrates us today results from manmade organizations, bureaucracies, and machines. What's important is not that you encounter frustration — that's a given — but how you handle it. Do you respond with curses, screams, and violence? Or with a deep breath, a silent prayer, and calm persistence and patience?

It may be difficult to imagine Jesus stuck in traffic or waiting for hours in a long line in a government office. It is not difficult, however, to imagine how he would act in such situations, and, thus, to know exactly how you should respond. No matter how frustrated you are.

*A life of frustration is inevitable for any coach whose main enjoyment is winning.*

*-- NFL Hall of Fame Coach Chuck Noll*

**Frustration is a vexing part of life,
but God expects us to handle it gracefully.**

# GREAT EXPECTATIONS

**Read John 1:43-51.**

*"'Nazareth! Can anything good come from there?'*
*Nathanael asked" (v. 46).*

**T**hey were disgusted -- totally.

Why? Because the man they had gathered to meet actually showed up, and he wasn't what they expected.

"They" were several hundred Auburn students, who were so keyed up about the arrival in 1904 of a new football coach they massed at the train station to welcome him. Auburn football needed a boost. After a 4-0 record in 1900, the team had gone 2-2-1 in 1901, 2-4-1 in 1902, and 4-3 in 1903.

And then the coach had to go and ruin everything by showing up. When the train pulled into the station "and the new coach set foot on Auburn soil for the first time," the students' jaws "went slack. The students stared at the coach, then they stared at each other."

The new coach was Mike Donahue, who called the students "the most disgusted bunch of people I've ever seen." There stood the new hope of Auburn football: all 5'4" of him with red hair and blue eyes, looking "more like some mother's son than a football coach. The students had expected a John Wayne. Instead, they had gotten a Mickey Rooney."

Most of us know something about failed expectations. The blind date, for instance, your friend promised would look like

Brad Pitt or Jennifer Aniston but resembled a Munster. Your vacation that went downhill after the lost luggage. Often your expectations are raised only to be dashed. Sometimes it's best not to get your hopes up; then at least you have the possibility of being surprised.

Worst of all, perhaps, is when you realize that you are the one not meeting others' expectations. The fact is, though, that you aren't here to live up to what others think of you. Jesus didn't; in part, that's why they killed him. But he did meet God's expectations for his life, which was all that really mattered.

Because God's kingdom is so great, God does have great expectations for any who would enter, and you should not take them lightly. What the world expects from you is of no importance; what God expects from you is paramount.

Mike Donahue, by the way, stepped off that "steaming, black train" that day and proceeded to lead Auburn to its first golden era in football. He coached through the 1922 season and had a 97-35-4 record at Auburn including one streak of 22-0-1 and four Southern Conference championships. He was Auburn's winningest coach until Shug Jordan came along.

Not bad for a Mickey Rooney.

*Other people may not have had high expectations for me, but I had high expectations for myself.*

*-- Gymnast Shannon Miller*

**You have little if anything to gain from meeting the world's expectations of you; you have all of eternity to gain from meeting God's.**

# IN THE BAD TIMES

### Read Philippians 1:3-14.

*"What has happened to me has really served to advance the gospel. . . . Most of the brothers in the Lord have been encouraged to speak the word of God more courageously and fearlessly" (vv. 12, 14).*

**D**iana Ramage was not your average Auburn golfer -- and it had nothing to do with how well she played, which was very well indeed.

As a senior in 2005, Ramage led the Tigers to the SEC championship and a third-place finish in the NCAA championships. She won the NCAA regional individual title, capping a career as an All-American and All-SEC golfer. She set the school records for lowest score over 18 holes and over 54 holes. After her career at Auburn, she turned pro.

But there's more to her game than just her remarkable shots.

When she was 15 and a sophomore in high school, Ramage was diagnosed with diabetes. "They did blood tests, and I left and came back later for the results," Ramage recalled. "I spent the next three days in the hospital getting poked with needles and educated about the disease."

Thus, at Auburn, Ramage always carried with her on the golf course the requisite supply of tees and balls as well as insulin, needles, a glucose monitor, and test strips. She wore an insulin pump all the time, receiving a shot of insulin every hour.

"As a player [Diana] is very persevering," Coach Kim Evans said during Ramage's senior season. "She always manages to get it done."

At first, Ramage was embarrassed by her illness. "I didn't want to be different," she said. "Thank God I'm over that. It's a pain, but I'm a lot better off than most. I just try to remember that I've been able to do what I want."

Loved ones die. You're downsized. Tests reveal you have diabetes. Your spouse could be having an affair. Hard, tragic times are as much a part of life as are breath and bad television.

This applies to Christians too. Faith in Jesus Christ does not exempt anyone from pain. Jesus promises he will be there for us to lead us through the valleys; he never promises that we will not enter them. The question therefore becomes how you handle the bad times. You can buckle to your knees in despair and cry, "Why me?" Or you can hit your knees in prayer and ask, "What do I do with this?"

Setbacks and tragedies are opportunities to reveal and to develop true character and abiding faith. Your faithfulness -- not your skipping merrily along through life without pain -- is what reveals the depth of your love for God.

*If I were to say, "God, why me?" about the bad things, then I should have said, "God, why me?" about the good things that happened in my life.*

*– Arthur Ashe*

**Faithfulness to God requires faith even in -- especially in -- the bad times.**

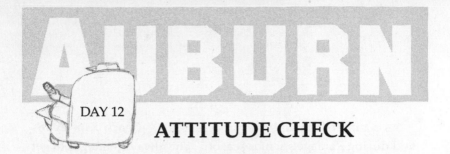

# ATTITUDE CHECK

**Read 1 Thessalonians 5.**

*"Give thanks in all circumstances, for this is God's will
for you in Christ Jesus" (v. 18).*

They weren't winning, they weren't whipping Alabama, and
they were on probation.

That was the unpromising situation in December 1992 when
Terry Bowden took over as head football coach at Auburn. All his
first team did was go 11-0, whip Florida 38-35 and Alabama 22-14,
and finish fourth in the nation.

How do you account for that?

What Bowden saw at Auburn was not a lack of talent. Better
players weren't the answer; what was needed was an attitude
adjustment by the ones on hand. So the rookie head coach set
about creating a positive attitude that was lacking after a 10-11-1
record over the last two seasons.

"You didn't have to say too much," Bowden said about those
early days. "When teams aren't doing well, the players will do
almost anything to win. You give them hope by giving them a
system and then bringing in people that they feel can lead them
to victory."

The sudden success all began, though, with an attitude
adjustment. A positive approach to the team's circumstances was
the theme for the 1993 season. Bowden figured the fans needed
to change their attitude, too, so in 1993 thousands of the Auburn

# TIGERS

faithful at the games sported lapel pins that emphasized their "Attitude."

The rest is Auburn lore. With new life from their positive approach, the Tigers won 20 straight games that included wins over top-ranked Florida in Gainesville and the almost mythological 30-26 shocker over LSU that featured three interceptions returned for touchdowns in the fourth quarter.

How's your attitude? You can fuss because your house is not as big as some, because a coworker talks too much, or because you have to take pills every day. Or you can appreciate your home for providing warmth and shelter, the co-worker for the lively conversation, and the medicine for keeping you reasonably healthy.

Whether life is endured or enjoyed depends largely on your attitude. An attitude of thankfulness to God offers you the best chance to get the most out of your life because living in gratitude means you choose joy in your life no matter what your circumstances.

This world does not exist to satisfy you, so chances are it will not. True contentment and joy are found in a deep, abiding relationship with God, and the proper way to approach God is not with haughtiness or anger but with gratitude for all he has given you.

*We just tried to create a positive attitude.*
*-- Terry Bowden on his first season at Auburn*

**Your attitude goes a long way**
**toward determining the quality of your life**
**and that of your relationship with God.**

# CUSS WORDS

### Read Psalm 10.

*"[The wicked man's] mouth is full of curses and lies and threats; trouble and evil are under his tongue" (v. 7).*

**C**harles Gibson, the last quarterback of the Mike Donahue era at Auburn, once tried to get thrown out of a game and couldn't.

"I didn't weigh but 146, and I wasn't a great ball carrier," Gibson recalled. "There was just one thing I could do, and that was block."

Gibson played in an age "of short rosters and long afternoons." 'If you started a game and didn't get killed, you finished it,'" Gibson said. Teams generally didn't have many players to platoon with. For instance, when Auburn played Army in 1922, only 18 players made the trip; the only substitution came with three minutes left in the game. "You played all the time," Gibson said, "but sometimes you would have liked to have gotten out."

One of those times was the 1922 game against Howard, which Auburn won 72-0 on the way to an 8-2 season. As the score mounted, Donahue began to substitute as much as he could -- except for Gibson. "Coach Donahue wanted me to stay in the game because it was my first year at quarterback and he wanted me to get the experience," Gibson explained.

But it was September, it was hot, Auburn was winning 55-0, and Gibson wanted out. So he decided that if the coach wouldn't take him out, he'd get thrown out. His strategy was to start

cussing. The referee responded with a warning: "Boy, if you don't hush that cussing, I'm going to put you out of the game." "Well, I started sure 'nuff then, 'cause that was what I wanted," Gibson recalled.

The ref never did send Gibson to an early shower. After the game, though, the official told Donahue, "Coach, you've got a good team, but you've got the cussingest quarterback I ever saw."

We live in a coarsened culture where words no one would utter in polite society a few decades ago now spew from our music and our television sets — and our own mouths.

Honestly answer these indelicate questions: With what name did you christen that slow driver you couldn't pass? What unflattering words did you have for that stubborn golf ball that wouldn't stay in the fairway? And what four-letter words do you sprinkle liberally in your conversations with people whom you want to think of you as "cool"?

Some argue that profane language is really harmless expression. It is in reality quite damaging, though, because of what its use reveals about the speaker: a lack of character, a lack of vocabulary, and a lack of respect for others and reverence for God.

The words you speak reveal what's in your heart, and what God seeks there is love and gentleness, not vileness.

*Don't cuss. Don't argue with the officials. And don't lose the game.*
                                        *-- Auburn Coach John Heisman*

**Our words -- including profane ones --
expose what's in our hearts.**

DAY 14

# KEEP OUT!

### Read Exodus 26:31-35; 30:1-10.

*"The curtain will separate the Holy Place from the Most Holy Place" (v. 26:33).*

No trespassing! Enter at your own risk!

You have been warned should you be foolish enough to enter the territory guarded by Marita Payne, a human wall where basketball shots went to die for four years at Auburn. She finished her career on The Plains in 2006 as the greatest shotblocker in Auburn women's basketball history. She played center for the Tigers at 6-foot-5, so she was naturally built to block shots and clog the lane.

But she worked hard at her craft. Before her senior season, she said, "I have worked hard in the summer to get my conditioning to a point to where I knew that I would be able to play as much as what they needed me to. I'm never going to be huge, but I definitely have worked on my strength."

Payne decided to leave home in Australia and play basketball in America simply because she loves the game. "I've always played to have fun," she explained. She particularly wanted to play in the fiercely competitive SEC, but the decision was still hard for her. "The main sacrifice was coming from another country and not being able to see your family and friends," she said.

Payne hit campus blocking shots. She set the school freshman record in 2002-03 with 47 blocks. She then broke the school

sophomore record with 73, which was also a new Auburn season record. That only set her up for an incredible junior season when she snuffed 141 shots, which led the nation and set an SEC single-season record. She also flew past Linda Godby's Auburn record of 199 career blocks. Another 116 rejections her senior season upped her career total to 377, good enough to make her the second-leading shot-blocker in SEC history.

Marita Payne issued no free passes.

That civic club with membership by invitation only. The bleachers where you sit while others frolic in the skyboxes. That neighborhood you can't afford a house in. You know all about being shut out of some club, some group, some place. "Exclusive" is the word that keeps you out.

The Hebrew people, too, knew about being told to keep out; only the priests could come into the presence of the holy and survive. Then along came Jesus to kick that barrier down and give us direct access to God.

In the process, though, Jesus created another exclusive club; its members are his followers, Christians, those who believe he is the Son of God and the savior of the world. This club, though, extends a membership invitation to everyone in the whole wide world; no one is excluded. Whether you're in or out depends on your response to Jesus, not on arbitrary gatekeepers.

*There are clubs you can't belong to, neighborhoods you can't live in, schools you can't get into, but the roads are always open.*

-- *Nike*

**Christianity is an exclusive club, but an invitation is extended to everyone and no one is denied entry.**

# PLAYING BY THE RULES

**Read Luke 6:1-11.**

*"They were furious and began to discuss with one another what they might do to Jesus" (v. 11).*

**N**o soap and hot water. No pork or pastry.

Those were among the rules legendary coach John Heisman had for his Auburn football players during his years on The Plains from 1895-99.

Heisman was a true eccentric, a Shakespearean actor who described a football to his players as a "prolate spheroid — that is, an elongated sphere — in which the outer leathern casing is drawn tightly over a somewhat smaller rubber tubing." "Thrust your projections into their cavities," he instructed his players on tackling, "grasping them about the knees and depriving them of their means of propulsion." He told his players, "Better to have died as a small boy than to fumble this football." He was also among football's pioneers, credited with bringing the forward pass to the game and inventing the hidden ball trick.

He declared that a football coach "should be masterful and commanding, even dictatorial. . . . At times he must be severe, arbitrary and little short of a czar." They weren't just idle words as he coached with a strict set of rules about the game and his players' conduct that would be unimaginable today.

For instance, he decreed that no two end runs should ever be run in succession and no pass should be thrown within 30

yards of your own goal. His teams were to punt on first down if they were close to their own goal. "When in doubt, punt anyway, anywhere," he declared. Among the "don'ts" the Auburn players saw on the locker room wall every day were these: "Don't have your feet in the way of the snapback"; "Don't forget to stiff-arm"; and "Don't go into the line with your head up."

Like Heisman's players, you live by rules others set up. Some lender determined the interest rate on your mortgage and your car loan. You work hours and shifts somebody else established. Someone else decided what day your garbage gets picked up and what school district your house is in.

Jesus encountered societal rules also, including a strict set that dictated what company he should keep, what people in other words, were fit for him to socialize with, talk to, or share a meal with. Jesus ignored the rules, choosing love instead and demonstrating both his love and his disdain for society's rules by mingling with the outcasts, the lowlifes, the poor, and the misfits.

You, too, have to choose when you find yourself in the presence of someone whom society deems undesirable. Will you choose the rules or love? Are you willing to be a rebel for love — as Jesus was?

*Play to win, observe the rules, and act like a gentleman.*
                        *-- Former basketball coach and author Clair Bee*

**Society's rules dictate who is acceptable
and who is not, but love in the name of Jesus
knows no such distinctions.**

# LANGUAGE BARRIER

**Read Mark 16:9-20.**

*"Go into all the world and preach the good news to all creation" (v. 13).*

Trivia time: Which of these is NOT a place where Auburn has played in a bowl game? Miami, New Orleans, Atlanta, Dallas, Pasadena, Tampa, or Havana? The answer? Pasadena. While the Tigers have never played in the Rose Bowl, they once played a bowl game in Havana, Cuba.

On Jan. 1, 1937, Auburn and Villanova tied 7-7 in the first and only Rhumba Bowl. The Cuban excursion into football was a feature of the first annual National Sports Festival.

The Tigers traveled to their first-ever bowl game by train to Tampa and by boat to Cuba, which caused some problems since most of the players had never been on a boat before. Trainer Wilbur Hustell loaded a bunch of oranges onto the boat, proclaiming they were good for seasickness. Nevertheless, five of the players, including quarterback Osmo Smith, made the trip leaning over the boat's rail. Tackle Bo Russell recalled that the Tigers still had the better of the trip: "Villanova came in . . . by plane and every one of those guys was sick as a dog."

The Cubans knew little about football and apparently cared even less. Despite predictions of a sellout, fewer than 9,000 folks showed up. The crowd got really excited about the game only during the couple of times "when fights broke out on the field, but

otherwise the whole thing was lost on the Cubans." The referees had to halt play once when two spectators with cameras showed up virtually in the Auburn backfield. "They were standing close enough to have caught the ball when it was snapped," recalled Joel Eaves, an All-SEC end that year.

As the Tigers' trip to Cuba illustrates, our games don't always translate across national and cultural boundaries. Language, though, is what usually erects a barrier to understanding. Recall your overseas vacation or your call to a tech support number when you got someone who spoke English but didn't understand it. Talking loud and waving your hands doesn't facilitate communication; it just makes you look weird.

Like many other aspects of life, faith has its jargon that can sometimes hinder understanding. Sanctification, justification, salvation, Advent, Communion with its symbolism of eating flesh and drinking blood – these and many other words have specific meanings to Christians that may be incomprehensible, confusing, and downright daunting to the newcomer or the seeker.

But the heart of Christianity's message centers on words that require no explanation: words such as hope, joy, love, purpose, and community. Their meanings are universal because people the world over seek them in their lives. Nobody speaks that language better than Jesus.

*Kindness is the universal language that all people understand.*
*-- Legendary Florida A&M Coach Jake Gaither*

**Jesus speaks across all language barriers**
**because his message of hope and meaning**
**resounds with people everywhere.**

# DOWNRIGHT CRAZY

**Read Luke 13:31-35.**

*"Some Pharisees came to Jesus and said to him, 'Leave this place and go somewhere else. Herod wants to kill you.' He replied, 'Go tell that fox . . . I must keep going today and tomorrow and the next day'" (vv. 31-33).*

**S**hug Jordan did a crazy thing – and the result was one of the greatest comebacks in Auburn football history.

On Nov. 6, 1954, at Legion Field, the sixth-ranked Miami Hurricanes led Auburn 13-0 with only 8:49 left to play. Despite Bobby Freeman's block of the second Miami extra point try, the Tigers were obviously in deep trouble.

That's when Jordan pulled what at the same seemed like a crazy stunt at worst, an exasperating ploy at best: He pulled some of his starters off the field to talk to them.

Jordan had something to say, though, that he felt merited having some of his best players on the sideline while the clock ticked on. Jordan told his team to hit the weak side of the Miami line, which was weak because the Canes were double- and triple-teaming Auburn's All-American end, Jim Pyburn.

The Tigers followed his advice and promptly drove 63 yards for a touchdown to make it 13-7. All-American fullback Joe Childress carried five straight times on the drive, scored, and then kicked the PAT. One writer said, "No fullback in the long history of Legion Field has ever dominated a football game like Childress

did."

Still, time was running out, so the Tigers needed a break. They got it when yet another All-American, tackle Frank D'Agostino, recovered a Cane fumble at the 27. Childress hit the weak side of the Miami line again, scored, and booted the extra point to give Auburn a 14-13 win and complete one of the greatest comebacks in Tiger football history.

And that comeback started because the coach did something downright crazy.

What some see as crazy often is shrewd instead. Like the time you went into business for yourself or when you decided to go back to school. Maybe it was when you fixed up that old house. Or when you invested in that new company's stock.

You know a good thing when you see it but are also shrewd enough to spot something that's downright crazy. Jesus was that way, too. He knew that entering Jerusalem was in complete defiance of all apparent reason and logic since a whole bunch of folks who wanted to kill him were waiting for him there.

Nevertheless, he went because he also knew that when the great drama had played out he would defeat not only his personal enemies but the most fearsome enemy of all: death itself.

It was, after all, a shrewd move that provided the way to your salvation.

*Football is easy if you're crazy.*

*-- Bo Jackson*

**It's so good it sounds crazy -- but it's not: through faith in Jesus, you can have eternal life with God.**

# PARTY TIME

**Read Exodus 14:26-31; 15:19-21.**

*"Miriam the prophetess, Aaron's sister, took a tambourine in her hand, and all the women followed her, with tambourines and dancing" (v. 15:20).*

It was a heck of a party -- and it was totally spontaneous.

On the night of Feb. 17, 1999, courtesy of the men's basketball team, Auburn fans threw one of their greatest parties ever. At Beard-Eaves Memorial Coliseum, the Tigers blasted Vanderbilt 81-63 to clinch the school's first SEC title since 1960.

The pandemonium and joy broke out before the game was over and began to build. "As the final seconds melted off the clock, the capacity crowd . . . was up and screaming, 'SEC! SEC! SEC!' When time ran out, students charged over the press table and past police to join the party on the floor." Coach Cliff Ellis personally saluted the rabid student section nicknamed the Cliff Dwellers. "The song 'We are the Champions' blared over the public address system. One by one, to roars from the crowd, Auburn players climbed a ladder and clipped off a piece of the net." When the Tigers ran to their dressing room, they passed through a phalanx of students and smiled, leaped, and slapped hands all the way.

"It was like a Hollywood gala," Ellis declared. "The stars came out." Some did for sure. Bo Jackson flew in from Chicago for the game; the governor was present to press the flesh.

It was quite a party all right for what many argue was the best

team in Auburn basketball history. They won their first 17 games and rose to No. 2 in the rankings. They went 29-4, a school record for wins, and at 14-2 in the conference won more SEC games than any team in school history.

But that party night was something special. "What better way to go out than, on your Senior Night, you win the SEC championship," said Bryant Smith, the player whom Ellis called the best leader he had ever seen.

You know what it takes to throw a good party. You start with your closest friends, add some salsa and chips, fire up the grill and throw on some burgers and dogs, and then top it all off with the Auburn game on TV.

You probably also know that any old excuse will do to get people together for a celebration. All you really need is a sense that life is pretty good right now.

That's the thing about having Jesus as part of your life: He turns every day into a celebration of the good life. No matter what tragedies or setbacks life may have in store, the heart given to Jesus will find the joy in living. That's because such a life is spent with quiet confidence in God's promise of salvation through Jesus, a confidence that inevitably bubbles up into a joy the world's troubles cannot touch.

The party never stops when a life is celebrated with Jesus!

*I don't think there's a senior across the nation happier than I am.*
*— Bryant Smith after defeating Vandy for the SEC title*

**With Jesus, life is one big party because it**
**becomes a celebration of victory and joy.**

# THE 'I' IN PRIDE

### Read 1 John 2:15-17.

*"Everything in the world -- the desire of the flesh, the desire of the eyes, the pride in riches -- comes not from the Father but from the world" (v. 16 NRSV).*

For Auburn football fans, Dec. 2, 1989, may still be the proudest moment in Tiger history. That's the day Alabama came to Jordan-Hare for the first time ever.

Coach Pat Dye understood the significance of the day. He recalled, "If you had walked down the street with me that day and looked in the eyes of mamas and daddies and brothers and sisters and grandmamas and granddaddies and saw what I saw -- the hunger in their eyes -- you would know what it meant to Auburn. It was a day for history."

David Housel, the school's sports information director, understood exactly what the day meant. He wrote in the game's souvenir program, "Today, for the first time, there is equality," between the Alabama and Auburn football programs. Wayne Hester, sports editor of *The Birmingham News*, wrote, "It was probably the most emotional day in Auburn football history."

Since the game was nationally televised, playing at Jordan-Hare put a regional and a national stamp onto the understanding that Auburn was no longer the state's football stepchild. And, oh yes, a game was played that day. Alabama was undefeated and ranked fourth; Auburn was 8-2 and ranked 10th. The Tigers

played up to the historic occasion, thumping Alabama 30-20. But Dye admitted that Alabama's "coming to Auburn was far more significant than the score of the game." It was, he said, "the most important thing that has happened since I've been here."

It was indeed a day for Auburn folks everywhere to be proud.

What are you most proud of? The size of your bank account? The trophies from your tennis league? The title under your name at the office? Your family?

Pride is one of life's great paradoxes. You certainly want a surgeon who takes pride in her work or an Auburn coach who is proud of his team's accomplishments. But pride in the things and the people of this world is inevitably disappointing because it leads to dependence upon things that will pass away and idolization of people who will fail you. Self-pride is even more dangerous because it inevitably leads to self-glorification.

Pride in the world's baubles and its people lures you to the earthly and the temporary and away from God and the eternal. Pride in yourself yields the same results in that you exalt yourself and not God.

God alone is glorious enough to be worshipped. Jesus Christ alone is Lord.


*After years of bondage, our people were finally delivered to the Promised Land.*
*-- Auburn AD David Housel after the 1989 Auburn-Alabama game*

**Pride can be dangerous because it tempts you**
**to lower your sight from God and the eternal**
**to the world and the temporary.**

# A HOLLYWOOD ENDING

**Read Luke 24:1-12.**

*"Why do you look for the living among the dead? He is not here; he has risen!" (vv. 5, 6a)*

**P**itch this to a Hollywood movie producer.

A top football team has more than one sensational running back, but the story isn't about them. It's about the guy who winds up so far down the depth chart that's he's never even started a game.

One running back quits the team. The starter breaks a leg. The replacement goes down with an ankle injury. That leaves only -- guess who? -- to start the game Saturday. Let make it THE game against arch-rival and hated Alabama in the Iron Bowl. And, oh, yeah, just for kicks, we'll make Alabama the top-ranked defense in the country. And we'll rank them in the top 10.

So what happens in the game? Hey, this is Hollywood. The fourth-string tailback rushes for 126 yards including a 51-yard run, the longest of his career, and leads the underdogs to a 17-7 win.

Think Hollywood would buy it? "If you were to write a script like that, you would laugh at it," Auburn coach Eddie Gran said. Only thing is -- it's true. The game was the 2002 Iron Bowl. The running back was Tre Smith, who became an instant Auburn legend in the first start of his career.

"A miracle" was how Coach Tommy Tuberville characterized

Smith's game.

"Everybody was talking junk, about me especially, and the rest of the running backs," Smith said after the game. But that was the problem: There weren't any more running backs. There was just Tre Smith, the unlikely hero in a game right out of Hollywood.

The world tells us that happy endings are for fairy tales and the movies, that reality is Cinderella dying in childbirth and her prince getting killed in a peasant uprising. But that's just another of the world's lies.

The truth is that Jesus Christ has been producing happy endings for almost two millennia. That's because in Jesus lies the power to change and to rescue a life no matter how desperate the situation. Jesus is the master at putting shattered lives back together, of healing broken hearts and broken relationships, of resurrecting lost dreams.

And as for living happily ever after – God really means it. The greatest Hollywood ending of them all was written on a Sunday morning centuries ago when Jesus left a tomb and death behind. With faith in Jesus, your life can have that same ending. You live with God in peace, joy, and love – forever.

The End.

*This field, this game, is a part of our past, Ray. It reminds us of all that once was good, and that could be again.*
                                    *-- James Earl Jones in* Field of Dreams

**Hollywood's happy endings are products
of imagination; the happy endings Jesus produces
are real and are yours for the asking.**

# FLAT BUSTED

### Read Luke 16:1-15.

*"You cannot serve both God and money" (v. 13b).*

**N**ot only did Shug Jordan not have many football players on hand when he took over as Auburn's head football coach in 1951 -- he didn't have any money to work with either.

The Tigers were coming off an 0-10 season in which they had been shut out seven times and had lost to Wofford and Southeast Louisiana. But the athletic department had a much more daunting problem than a losing streak: It was flat busted, broke. "We didn't have a nickel," newly appointed athletic director Jeff Beard recalled. Actually, the situation was worse than that: Auburn's athletic department was $100,000 in debt. "We bought our uniforms on credit. That's how bad it was," Beard said.

Beard and Jordan didn't have a huge facility into which they could jam ticket-buying fans either; they had only 7,500 concrete seats at their disposal in Cliff Hare Stadium.

Nevertheless, Beard came up with an idea. Since schedules weren't made up years in advance in those days, he proposed opening the 1951 season with a barnburner that would draw a good crowd. He got Vanderbilt, one of the South's finest programs at the time, to come to Auburn to inaugurate the Shug Jordan era.

About 17,000 fans paid $2.50 per ticket and packed the concrete seats, all the temporary seats Beard could find, and what

he called the "Bermuda seats": some seats on the grass. When the Tigers upset the Commodores 24-14, the renewal of Auburn's football fortunes had begun, not just on the field but in the ledger book also. "That was the turning point," Beard said. "Shug's first victory."

In three years, the athletic department was $250,000 in the black and the football team was winning.

Having a little too much money at the end of the month may be as bothersome -- if not as worrisome -- as having a little too much month at the end of the money. The investment possibilities are bewildering: stocks, bonds, mutual funds, that group pooling their money to open up a neighborhood coffee shop -- that's a good idea.

You take your money seriously, as well you should. Jesus, too, took money seriously, warning us frequently of its dangers. Money itself is not evil; its peril lies in the ease with which it can usurp God's rightful place as the master of our lives.

Certainly in our age and society, we often measure people by how much money they have. But like our other talents, gifts, and resources, money should primarily be used for God's purposes. God's love must touch not only our hearts but our wallets also.

How much of your wealth are you investing with God?

*Money can buy you everything but happiness. It can pay your fare to everywhere but heaven.*
                                                    *-- Pete Maravich*

**Your attitude about money says much
about your attitude toward God.**

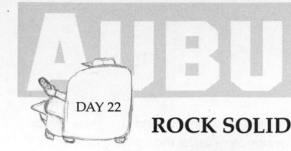

# ROCK SOLID

**Read Luke 6:46-49.**

*"I will show you what he is like who comes to me and hears my words and puts them into practice. He is like a man building a house, who dug down deep and laid the foundation on rock" (vv. 47-48).*

**H**er jersey has never been retired. She never made All-SEC or All-America. She never played on an Olympic team. She didn't even get a scholarship out of high school.

Yet she may well be the greatest women's basketball player in Auburn history.

Consider these staggering statistics: She holds the Auburn record for the highest scoring average in a season (21.9) and the highest career average (20.4). She holds the school record for the highest rebounding average in a season (15.3), the most rebounds in a game (26), and the highest career rebounding average (10.0). She is third all-time in career points scored, more than Carolyn Jones and the Bolton sisters, and fifth all-time in career rebounds.

So who is this player and why isn't she recognized and honored?

She is Marianne Merritt, whose fate it was to come along too early. She finished her remarkable career at Auburn in 1979, before women's games were televised, before they were part of the NCAA, before the SEC recognized the game, before Joe Ciampi arrived on campus and began to build a championship program.

"It was very different," Merritt recalled. "We had nothing. We drove our own cars to games. There wasn't all the money that goes into the program now." Neatly summarizing her place in history, Merritt said, "I think I played too early."

She played simply for the love of the game, before the glory days of Auburn women's basketball, but she helped lay the foundation for those players who came later.

Like women's basketball at Auburn, your life is an ongoing project, a work in progress. As with any complex construction job, if your life is to be stable, it must have a solid foundation that holds everything up and keeps everything together.

R. Alan Culpepper said in *The New Interpreter's Bible*, "We do not choose whether we will face severe storms in life; we only get to choose the foundation on which we will stand." In other words, tough times are inevitable. If your foundation isn't rock-solid, you will have nothing on which to stand as those storms buffet you, nothing to keep your life from flying apart into a cycle of disappointment and destruction.

But when the foundation is solid and sure, you can take the blows, stand strong, recover, and live with joy and hope. Only one foundation is sure and foolproof: Jesus Christ. Everything else you build upon will fail you.

*When I was younger, I thought that the key to success was just hard work. But the real foundation is faith.*
*-- Former NFL player Howard Twilley*

**In the building of your life, you must start
with a foundation in Jesus Christ, or the first
trouble that shows up will knock you down.**

# BATTLE OF THE HOOCH

**Read Hebrews 12:14-17.**

*"Make every effort to live in peace with all men and to be holy" (v. 14).*

The Battle of Chattahoochee.

That's what one sportswriter dubbed the fight that broke out in the 1956 football game against Georgia, which was played in Columbus.

Auburn led 14-0 on the way to a 20-0 win when the Tigers intercepted a pass to stop a Georgia threat. Everybody's attention was downfield on the play -- at least for a moment. That changed quickly as back behind the line of scrimmage Auburn guard Tim Baker, who was to captain the 1957 national championship team, was embroiled in an all-out brawl with several Georgia players.

On the play, Baker had gotten past a Georgia lineman named Harold Cook to pressure the quarterback and had been blocked by the halfback. As Baker recalled it, "Cook got up, came back there and started a fight with me. Everybody else had gone downfield with the pass, but there we were, Cook, me, the quarterback, the halfback, fighting like cats and dogs."

The Auburn players quickly headed back upfield to aid their outnumbered teammate, and the benches emptied. Baker said, "I can still see Coach [Shug] Jordan and all the boys coming out." The melee spread as "fights broke out all over the field" while cops and coaches tried to pull players apart. Order was restored

only when the Auburn band struck up the national anthem.

While Baker was exonerated of being the instigator of the Battle of Chattahoochee and was strenuously defended by Jordan, he nevertheless "did not shirk any front-line trench duty. He went into the midst of the action and . . . used a little subtle persuasion against the enemy."

Baker is "a football player, not a fighter," Jordan said in his final comment about the Battle of the Hooch.

Perhaps you've never been in a brawl or a public brouhaha to match that of Tim Baker and his Auburn teammates. But maybe you retaliated when you got one elbow too many in a pickup basketball game. Or maybe you and your spouse or your teenager get into it occasionally, shouting and saying cruel things. Or road rage may be a part of your life.

While we do seem to live in a more belligerent, confrontational society than ever before, fighting is still not the solution to a problem. It only escalates the whole confrontation, leaving wounded pride, intransigence, and simmering hatred in its wake. Actively seeking and making peace is the way to a solution that lasts and heals.

Peacemaking is not as easy as fighting, but it is much more courageous and a lot less painful. It is also the Jesus thing to do.

*No matter what the other fellow does on the field, don't let him lure you into a fight. Uphold your dignity.*
*-- Alabama Coach Frank Thomas*

**Making peace instead of fighting takes courage and strength; it's also what Jesus would do.**

# HOMEMAKER

### Read Joshua 24:14-27.

*"Choose for yourselves this day whom you will serve. . . .
But as for me and my household, we will serve the Lord"
(v. 15).*

**A** home-field advantage in *lacrosse?*

Hey, this is Auburn, where no matter what the sport, the fans' vocal and passionate support of their beloved Tigers gives the teams a home-field advantage. Even in lacrosse.

In April 2003 the Florida Gators came to town, and despite some foul, rainy weather, Tiger fans turned out to cheer for their two-time Southeastern champions while relishing the chance to taunt and goad the opponents.

As it turned out, they were very good at it. They were so good, in fact, that at one point the officials called time out to remove some vociferous fans from the Florida sidelines to keep them from taunting and baiting the Gators.

It didn't work. An upset Florida coach continued to complain about Auburn's rowdy and "over enthusiastic fans" over on the opposite sideline. One referee finally turned to the coach and said in exasperation, "When you're playing here, what do you expect, coach?" Seems the reputation of Auburn's lacrosse fans preceded them.

The Auburn faithful know they can make a difference by urging the Tigers on and by disturbing the poise of the visitors. Nothing

can engender panic in a struggling team like the roar of tens of thousands of zealous folks in Jordan-Hare or some pointed and disquieting barbs lobbed by "over enthusiastic" and quite expert Auburn lacrosse fans.

Whether it's a condo, an apartment, a two-story mansion, a sprawling ranch house, or a country place with a wraparound porch, you know it as home. It's much more than a place to hang out for a while before you crash.

You enter to find love, security, and joy. It is the place where your heart feels warmest, your laughter comes easiest, and your life is its richest. It is the center of and the reason for everything you do and everything you are.

How can a home be such a place?

If it is a home where grace is spoken before every meal, it is such a place. If it is a home where the Bible is read, studied, and discussed by the whole family gathered together, it is such a place. If it is a home that serves as a jumping-off point for the whole family to go to church, not just on Sunday morning and not just occasionally, but regularly, it is such a place. If it is a home where the name of God is spoken with reverence and awe and not with disrespect and indifference, it is such a place. In other words, a house becomes a true home when God is part of the family.

*Having a home away from the media glare is important to the world-class athlete.*

-- *Mary Lou Retton*

**A home is full when all the family members
are present -- including God.**

# SOUTHERN HOSPITALITY

**Read 2 Kings 4:8-17.**

*"Let's make a small room on the roof and put in it a bed and a table, a chair and a lamp for him. Then he can stay there whenever he comes to us" (v. 10).*

It's only a little more than 300 miles from Knoxville to Auburn -- but it took the Tennessee football team 74 years to make the trip.

Auburn and Tennessee first met in football in 1900 with Auburn winning easily 23-0. They did not play again until 1929 and then met five times in the 1930s before beginning what became an annual bloodletting in 1956. One thing was constant about all those Auburn-Tennessee games from 1900 to 1974: None of them were played in Auburn. The contract specified that the games would be played in Knoxville and Birmingham because of the small size of Auburn's stadium. Not until 1974 did the Tigers host the Vols for the first time.

Coach Shug Jordan took advantage of the situation to motivate his team. Quarterback Phil Gargis recalled Jordan told the Tigers, "This is our home; this is our house. Protect it like you would your own." Gargis said Jordan's speech hit home with the team: "We took pride in Jordan-Hare Stadium."

Their pride showed as they did indeed defend their home turf with a vengeance against the invading Volunteers. In fact, the Tigers were downright rude hosts as they used their dives and options to stomp the favored Volunteers 21-0 behind three touch-

downs by reserve fullback Kenny Burks. Alf Van Hoose of *The Birmingham News* wrote that the Vols were annihilated, devastated, humiliated, and "whipped every way known to Tigers."

Still, Auburn managed to show a little graciousness as Tennessee's long day wound down. At the end of the game, the public address announcer intoned to dejected Vol fans, "It's been nice to have you in Auburn." Nice indeed.

Southerners are deservedly famous for their hospitality. Down South, warmth and genuineness seem genetic. You open your home to the neighborhood kids, to your friends, to the stranger whose car broke down in the rain, to the stray cat that showed up hungry and hollering. You even let family members overstay their welcome without grumbling.

Hospitality was vital to the cultures of Biblical times also. Travelers faced innumerable dangers: everything from lions to bandits to deadly desert heat. Finding a temporary haven thus often became quite literally a matter of life and death.

Since hospitality has through the ages been a sign of a loving and generous nature, it is not surprising that almighty God himself is a gracious host. He welcomes you, not as a stranger, but as an adopted child. One glorious day this hospitable God will open the doors of his place for you -- and never ask you to leave.

*Being raised in the South means growing up on a diet of southern hospitality and a dose of football every weekend.*

*– Askman.com*

**Hospitality is an outward sign of the inward loving, generous, and godly nature of the host.**

# TEARS TO TRIUMPH

**Read Matthew 27:45-50, 55-61.**

*"Many women were there, watching from a distance. They had followed Jesus from Galilee to care for his needs" (v. 55).*

**Y**ou're on the verge of losing yet another football game in a long season -- and you remember it as one of the greatest moments of your life?

That's the way it was for Gabe Gross. Gross was one of Auburn's greatest baseball players. He hit .363 as a freshman leftfielder and then topped that as a sophomore with one of the greatest seasons in Auburn baseball history when he hit .430 with 13 home runs. After his junior season in 2001, he was the fifteenth player drafted, and he made his major-league debut on Aug. 7, 2004, for the Toronto Blue Jays at Yankee Stadium.

Gross also played quarterback until three games into the 1999 season he gave up football to concentrate on baseball. On Oct. 31, 1998, he was the starter for the Tigers against Arkansas. Midway through the season, head coach Terry Bowden had resigned, replaced by interim coach Bill Oliver. Auburn was struggling with a 2-5 record while the Razorbacks rolled into Jordan-Hare with a gaudy 7-0 record.

The Tigers played their hearts out, but it wasn't enough. His final pass incomplete, Gross stood on the sidelines watching Arkansas run out the clock to win 24-21. Nothing to do but hang

your head, right? Hey, this is Auburn.

"It started kind of slowly," Gross remembered. "It picked up and picked up. Pretty soon, everybody wearing blue and orange in that stadium was yelling 'It's great to be an Auburn Tiger.' We were getting ready to lose our sixth game, but it was still great to be an Auburn Tiger."

A time of bitter defeat was transformed into a moment of overarching triumph.

We all have times of defeat and loss in our lives, but nothing fills us with such an overwhelming sense of helplessness as the death of a loved one. There's absolutely nothing you can do about it. Like the women who stood at a distance and watched Jesus die on the darkest, bleakest day in history, you, too, can only stand helpless and weep as something precious and beautiful leaves your life.

For the believer in Jesus Christ and his loved ones, though, the Sunday of resurrection – the grandest, most triumphant day in history – follows the Friday of death. Faith in Jesus transforms loss into triumph, not only for the loved one but for those left behind. Amid your tears and your sense of loss, you celebrate the ultimate victory of your family member or friend. Amid death, you find life; amid sorrow, you find hope.

What a way to die! What a way to live!

*I know when I wake up that ultimately my steps are ordered by the Lord.*

– *Gabe Gross*

**Faith in Jesus Christ transforms death
from the ultimate defeat to the ultimate victory.**

# AT THE LAST TRUMPET

**Read 1 Corinthians 15:50-58.**

*"The trumpet will sound, the dead will be raised imperishable, and we will be changed" (v. 52).*

Levorn "Porkchop" Harbin was the human wake-up call.

Harbin was a graduate assistant during the 1999 and 2000 football seasons whose primary responsibility was to make sure the players got out of the bed in the morning and made it to class on time. Exactly how did "Porkchop" come by his unusual nickname? Coach Tommy Tuberville simply decided that Harbin needed one, and he became "Porkchop."

Harbin, who played for Division II national champion North Alabama in 1995, was in charge of about 30 players in Sewell Hall. He woke them up each morning at 7:00 so they could make it to the cafeteria by 7:30 for breakfast and class. If they didn't, they wound up with extra running or other equally less enticing ways to spend their time.

As you would expect, Porkchop heard his share of excuses and developed his own techniques to counter them. "Sometimes kids like to tell their coaches that they didn't hear me knock," Harbin said, "but I kick that door real rude. And if that don't get them up, I got a key to get in their room. I just kind of go in and turn the lights on and start yelling and all. Shaking them up."

Porkchop's tool of last resort was a bullhorn. "With the real heavy sleepers, I open the door and I just blow the horn in

the room," he said. "I'm not their favorite person," Porkchop conceded.

"When I first came in," Porkchop recalled, "they didn't like me. But it's different now, since they know that I'm doing it because I care, and I'm fair about it regardless of who you are."

When Porkchop Harbin showed up, it was getting-up time.

Being roused out of bed in the morning – by a bullhorn or by something a mite gentler -- may not be among the great joys of your life. You may well agree that the alarm clock is numbered among history's most sadistic inventions.

But one day you will be awakened by a trumpet shrieking in your ear – and you will be overjoyed about it. The Hebrew people of the Bible knew about the good news signaled by a trumpet blast because the sounding of the trumpets announced the start of the great festivals and other extraordinary events. Trumpets blown by the priests controlled and coordinated the march of the people to the Promised Land and reminded them that God watched over them.

The day will come when the last trumpet will sound in the final and true wake-up call. On that day, with that blast, Jesus will summon the faithful to paradise. No one will ever need an alarm clock – or a bullhorn -- again.

*He's a guy who gets up at six o'clock in the morning regardless of what time it is.*

*– Boxing trainer Lou Duva*

**God will sound a final wake-up call
at which even the sleepiest will arise.**

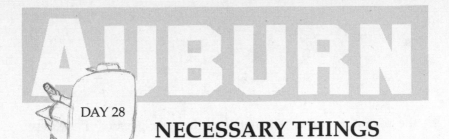

# NECESSARY THINGS

**Read Luke 18:18-29.**

*"You still lack one thing. Sell everything you have and give to the poor, and you will have treasure in heaven. Then come, follow me" (v. 22).*

**T**he ladies were fine; football was a problem.

That was the situation at Auburn in 1892, when two glorious institutions arrived on campus: coeds and football. Football's problem was that it was losing money. The solution was obvious: play that new team over there, the one from the University of Alabama.

A game was scheduled for February 22, 1893, at Lakeview Park in Birmingham. The game immediately caught the state's fancy.

*The Birmingham Daily News* covered the festivities extensively, telling of the arrival of the spectators, how they acted, and how they dressed. Careful to remain neutral, the reporter said fans and students "presented a handsome appearance. . . . Both Universities brought a charming set of young ladies with them."

The paper detailed the security measures (Chief Norton and four officers), the colors of the team uniforms, and the arrangements for the parking of carriages (on the east side of the field). The article duly noted the dismay of some of the female fans at the ruggedness of the pre-game practice: "The ladies would get alarmed, fearing that [the players] would have their bones broken, but their gentlemen friends would kindly assure the timid sympa-

thetic women that the athletic youths could be dropped from the top of the grandstand without sustaining any injury."

The reporter produced a colorful story that was, however, noticeably short on details of the game. He didn't give the score, how the teams scored, or who did what. He left out everything that was necessary to a good story about the game.

It's possible to omit the necessary things in life too. Like the ruler who approached Jesus, we clutter our lives with things, with trinkets, with toys; we surround ourselves with stuff.

We take up the days of our lives with quite legitimate work: making a living, paying the bills, maintaining a home, taking care of the kids, planning for the future. But in staying so busy we often allow ourselves to omit in our lives what is truly necessary and precious.

Nothing is more necessary or more important in our lives than God and our relationship with him. Thus, the necessary things in our life include learning God's truth and growing as a Christian, loving not just our family members but those around us and reaching out to them with the truth of Jesus' salvation, and obeying God's word in our lives.

No matter how full it may seem, a life without God and Jesus is empty.

*From what we get, we can make a living; what we give, however, makes a life.*

*-- Arthur Ashe*

**Material wealth, possessions, and busy schedules can clutter a life, but they can never fill it.**

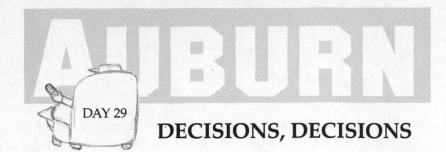

# DECISIONS, DECISIONS

**Read John 6:60-69.**

*"The words I have spoken to you are spirit and they are life. Yet there are some of you who do not believe" (vv. 63b-64a).*

**A**shley Moore knew nothing about the fierce Auburn-Alabama rivalry when she moved to Birmingham from Stamford, Conn. -- but it didn't take her long to find out.

Moore arrived in Alabama as a second-grader. She said, "The kids all asked me on the first day [of school] who I was for? I was like, 'What do you mean who am I for?' They said 'Auburn or Alabama.' I went home that night and asked my dad who we were for. He said to just choose one, so I chose Auburn."

And what was the basis for such a momentous decision? "I liked their colors better."

Several years later, Moore had to choose again between Auburn and Alabama. She was a high school softball star and had scholarship offers from both. Once again, she decided for Auburn, coming to The Plains to play softball in 1998 when the school's program was just in its third year.

She left as one of the greatest players in Auburn history. She set a school record her senior year with 17 home runs and helped lead the Tigers to their first NCAA regional. When she left in 2002, she had a career batting average of .341 and set school career records for hits, doubles, and runs. She finished second only to

Mary Petrie in career home runs and RBI's.

Since she excelled at the game, surely Moore's initial decision to play high school softball rather than soccer, at which she also was a star, came after measured and deliberate consideration. Nope. She chose softball because her older brother had played baseball. "I always wanted to be just like him," she said.

The moment to which you have arrived in your life – this time, this place, this situation right now – is the result of the decisions you have made. Some you made suddenly and frivolously as second-grader Ashley Moore did in picking Auburn; some you made carefully and deliberately; some were forced upon you.

Perhaps decisions made for frivolous reasons have determined how your life unfolds, and you may have discovered that some of those spur-of-the-moment decisions have turned out better than your carefully considered ones.

Of all your life's decisions, however, none is more important than one you cannot ignore: What have you done with Jesus? Even in his time, people chose to follow Jesus or to reject him, and nothing has changed; the decision must still be made and nobody can make it for you.

Carefully considered or spontaneous – how you arrive at a decision for Jesus doesn't matter; all that matters is that you get there.

*If you're from Alabama you're either for the University of Alabama or you're for Auburn. And once you move here, you're asked to declare.*
*– Auburn radio announcer Jim Fyffe*

**A decision for Jesus may be spontaneous or considered; what counts is that you make it.**

# SOUTHERN GENTLEMAN

**Read John 2:13-22.**

*"He made a whip out of cords, and drove all from the temple area . . .; he scattered the coins of the money changers and overturned their tables" (v. 15).*

**H**e was a "courtly Southern gentleman."

At least that's what the sportswriters thought of legendary Auburn football coach Shug Jordan. Jordan's wife, Evelyn, backed up that image. She once said, "Shug's saddest times were over injuries. He could walk in the house after practice and I could tell if somebody had gotten hurt."

How could such a gentleman survive in the rough-and-tumble and downright cutthroat SEC? More than that, how could such a gentleman succeed? Jordan certainly succeeded. He coached Auburn for 25 years (1951-75) and retired with 176 wins, the most of any coach in Auburn football history. He won a national championship, an SEC championship, and national and SEC coach-of-the-year honors, and coached twelve bowl teams, twenty All-Americas, and one Heisman Trophy winner. In 1982, he was inducted posthumously into the College Football Hall of Fame.

How can we explain this apparent paradox? The confusion arises only if we mistakenly confuse "gentleman" with "soft." Jordan was a gentleman, but he was not soft. As a lieutenant, he took part in four major Allied invasions in World War II, including Normandy. His steely demeanor and full measure of backbone

were exemplified by his reaction when his alma mater hired a coach from Notre Dame in 1947 instead of him: "If they don't think an Auburn man can do the job, they ought to close the joint down." He once defended himself by growling, "At least I don't climb up in a four-story tower and holler through a bullhorn like a plantation owner working slaves."

A calm, caring manner and a soft voice are often taken for weakness, and gentle men are frequently misunderstood by those who fail to appreciate their inner strength. But Shug Jordan's coaching career and Jesus' rampage through the Jerusalem temple illustrate the perils of underestimating a determined gentleman.

A gentleman treats other people kindly, respectfully, and justly, and conducts himself ethically in all situations. A gentleman doesn't lack resolve or backbone. Instead, he determines to live in a way that is exceedingly difficult in our selfish, me-first society; he lives the lifestyle God desires for us all.

Included in that mode of living is the understanding that the best way to have a request honored is to make it civilly, with a smile. God works that way too. He could bully you and boss you around; you couldn't stop him. But instead, he gently requests your attention and politely waits for the courtesy of a reply.

*Coach Shug Jordan was a true gentleman, but he had a mean, cold streak to do what he had to do.*
*-- Auburn defensive end Liston Eddings*

**God is a gentleman, soliciting your attention**
**politely and then patiently waiting for you**
**to give him the courtesy of a reply.**

# JOY JUMPING

**Read Luke 6:20-26.**

*"Rejoice in that day and leap for joy, because great is your reward in heaven" (v. 23).*

**E**va Goulbourne is the greatest jumper in Auburn history.

The Jamaican native totally dominated the jumping events in college track and field for the two seasons she was at Auburn. In 2002 and 2003, she won five NCAA championships, the most in Auburn history.

"Growing up, I was always running ahead of everyone," Goulbourne said. "I was always good at school, especially at math, and I was always strong and fast."

Her coach at Auburn, Ralph Spry, called the 2003 NCAA Indoor Championships "the Eva Goulbourne show." Against the best the nation had to offer, Goulbourne was so good that she competed in the triple jump for just the second time in her life and won the national championship.

How dominating was she? Auburn as a team scored 29 points in those championships; Goulbourne had 28 of them. She was honored as the 2003 Trackshark Indoor Female Athlete of the Year and was named the Southeastern Conference Female Athlete of the Year for indoor track.

In 2002, she won the SEC outdoor long jump by flying more than a foot longer than her nearest competitor. Her leap broke the Auburn school record by more than six inches.

That same year she won the NCAA long jump championship both indoors and outdoors. She followed that up by winning both championships again in 2003, plus that surprising triple jump. Goulbourne confessed that she didn't expect to win the triple jump. "I was very surprised," she said. "I told my coaches to let me compete in the event because I can hop, skip and jump. I never thought I would win the national championship."

You're probably a pretty good jumper yourself when the Tigers score against Alabama, Georgia, or LSU. You just can't help it. It's like your feet and your seat have suddenly become magnets that repel each other. The sad part is that you always come back down to earth; the moment of exultation passes.

But what if you could jump for joy all the time? Not literally, of course; you'd pass out from exhaustion. But figuratively, with your heart aglow and joyous even when life is its most difficult.

Joy is an absolutely essential component of the Christian life. Not only do we experience joy in our public praise and worship – which is temporary – but we live daily in the joy that comes from the presence of God in our lives and the surety of his saving power extended to us through Jesus Christ.

It's not happiness, which derives from external factors; it's joy, which comes from inside.

*You can't even jump high enough to touch the rim unless they put a Big Mac on it.*

*-- Charles Barkley to Arkanssas' Oliver Miller*

**Unbridled joy can send you jumping all over the place; life in Jesus means such exultation is not rare but rather is a way of life.**

DAY 32

# UNEXPECTEDLY

**Read Luke 2:1-20.**

*"She gave birth to her firstborn, a son. She wrapped him in cloths and placed him in a manger, because there was no room for them in the inn" (v. 7).*

Some bad scores: 7-0. 33-7. 68-7. 41-0.

Those were the scores by which Auburn had lost four straight to former coach John Heisman's Golden Tornado of Georgia Tech when the two teams took to the field in the final game of the 1919 season. At one point, Auburn had led in the series 15-1-1 and had massacred Tech 94-0 in 1894, 45-0 in 1896, 63-0 in 1899, and 44-0 in 1908. But things had turned around, and they weren't expected to change in 1919.

Auburn had lost only one game that season, 7-6 to Vanderbilt on a return of a blocked punt and a fumble at the Vandy two. Nevertheless, the Tigers were heavy underdogs in the game in Atlanta that would decide the Southern championship before the largest crowd in Southern football history. *Atlanta Journal* Sports Editor Morgan Blake wrote, "All indications point to a fifth straight victory by Tech Thursday by a margin of from three to five touchdowns."

Blake had no future as a prophet. Tech scored on the game's sixth play to lead 7-0, but after that the game belonged completely to Auburn. All-Southern lineman Pete Bonner blocked a punt that John Sloan carried in for a 35-yard touchdown, and C.C.

Warren took a Tech fumble 45 yards for a touchdown as Mike Donahue's Tigers claimed the championship of the South with a 14-7 win. *The Birmingham News* said the upset "turned the old town upside down" and "the golden youths from the Plains of Auburn celebrated all night." Perhaps still dazed a few days later, Blake wrote, "A thunderbolt crashed out of a clear sky Thursday and the thunderbolt was Auburn. . . . Ye Gods!"

The unexpected is "a bolt out of the blue," speaking of the unpredictability of life, the power of a lightning bolt, and the workings of a divine presence. Someone gets ill; you fall in love; you lose your job; you're going to have another child. Life surprises us with its bizarre twists and turns.

God is that way too, catching us unawares to remind us he's still around. A friend who hears you're down and stops by, a child's laugh, an achingly beautiful sunset -- unexpected moments of love and beauty. God is like that, always doing something in our lives we didn't expect.

But why shouldn't he? There is nothing God can't do. The only factor limiting what God can do is the paucity of our own faith.

Expect the unexpected from God, this same deity who unexpectedly came to live among us as a man. He does, by the way, expect a response from you.

*There's one word that describes baseball: You never know.*
                                                              *-- Yogi Berra*

**God does the unexpected to remind you
of his presence -- like showing up as Jesus --
and now he expects a response from you.**

# AMAZING!

**Read: Luke 4:31-36.**

*"All the people were amazed and said to each other, "What is this teaching? With authority and power he gives orders to evil spirits and they come out!"" (v. 36)*

They were amazin', the bunch Coach Shug Jordan claimed was one of his favorite teams.

"The biggest change in the Southeastern Conference power structure will be the demise of Auburn." So opined one writer about the 1972 football team, generally picked to finish seventh in the conference. Instead, they amazed everyone, going 9-1 against what some called the toughest schedule in the country, whipping favored Colorado 24-3 in the Gator Bowl, and finishing no. 5 in the country.

The Amazin's didn't score a lot, but they could play defense and they could come up with a big play with the likes of defensive backs Johnny Simmons and Dave Beck, tailback Terry Henley, and quarterback Randy Walls. Some of the scores from that season indicate a time in college football when defenses dominated: 14-7 over Chattanooga, 14-3 over Miss. State, 10-6 over Tennessee.

The season also featured what is almost certainly the most amazing game in Auburn's long and storied football history. Against second-ranked and undefeated Alabama, Auburn blocked two kicks and scored 17 points in the last 9:15 of the game to stun the Tide 17-16.

# TIGERS

Bama led 16-3 when Bill Newton and David Langner etched their names into the Auburn history books and the hearts and minds of Auburn fans forever. Newton blocked a punt, Langner scooped up the loose ball and scored – twice.

The most amazing game in Auburn football history capped off an amazing season.

The word *amazing* defines the limits of what you believe to be plausible or usual. The Grand Canyon, the birth of your children, those last-second Auburn wins and upsets -- they're amazing!

Some people in Galilee felt the same way when they encountered Jesus. Jesus amazed them with the authority of his teaching, and he wowed them with his power over spirit beings. People everywhere just couldn't quit talking about him.

It would have been amazing had they not been amazed. They were, after all, witnesses to the most amazing spectacle in the history of the world: God himself was right there among them walking, talking, teaching, preaching, and healing.

Their amazement should be a part of your life too because Jesus still lives. The almighty and omnipotent God of the universe seeks to spend time with you every day – because he loves you. Amazing!

*It's amazing. Some of the greatest characteristics of being a winning football player are the same ones it's true to be a Christian man.*
*                                                                  -- Bobby Bowden*

**Everything about God is amazing,**
**but perhaps most amazing of all**
**is that he loves us and desires our company.**

# PAIN RELIEF

**Read 2 Corinthians 1:3-7.**

*"Just as the sufferings of Christ flow over into our lives, so also through Christ our comfort overflows" (v. 5).*

As Stacy Danley lay on the ground after a vicious hit, Coach Pat Dye went to him on the field while television commentators praised this demonstration of how much he cared for his players. They were clueless.

The Tigers met Ohio State in the Hall of Fame Bowl in Tampa after the 1989 season. Auburn finished the regular season 9-2, grabbing a share of their third straight SEC championship. They beat LSU, Florida, Georgia, and Alabama along the way. The team had its share of stars: All-American linebacker Craig Ogletree, quarterback Reggie Slack, tailback Stacy Danley, wide receiver Alexander Wright, center John Hudson, and offensive tackle Bob Meeks among others.

But they were struggling in the bowl game with Ohio State leading 14-10 in the third quarter. That's when Danley got flattened and the game turned around. Dye did indeed come out to check on his prostrate player, but the coach wasn't there to comfort him. "He hated for guys to lie around on the field," Danley recalled, laughing at the memory.

Danley said the head coach "asked the trainer if I was going to be OK. Really, I'd just had the wind knocked out of me." Then Dye "looked down at me and said 'You get up and run . . . off the

field and don't let those son of a guns know they hurt you.' . . . When he said that, the breath kind of came back. I got up and ran off the field like he said. People said that was the turning point of the game."

From that point on, the game belonged to Auburn. Slack threw for two touchdowns and ran for another in the second half. Danley wound up with 85 yards on 20 carries. The Tigers routed the Buckeyes 31-14.

And it all started with a little pain.

Since you live on earth and not in heaven, you are forced to play with pain. Whether it's a car wreck that left you shattered, the end of a relationship that left you battered, or a loved one's death that left you tattered -- pain finds you and challenges you to keep going.

While God's word teaches that you will reap what you sow, life also teaches that pain and hardship are not necessarily the result of personal failure. Pain in fact can be one of the tools God uses to mold your character and change your life.

What are you to do when you are hit full-speed by the awful pain that seems to choke the very will to live out of you? Where is your consolation, your comfort, and your help?

In almighty God, whose love will never fail. When life knocks you to your knees, you're closer to God than ever before.

*It hurts up to a point and then it doesn't get any worse.*
-- *Ultramarathon runner Ann Trason*

**When life hits you with pain, you can always turn to God for comfort, consolation, and hope.**

# ROLLING THE TREES

**Read Luke 15:1-10.**

*"There is rejoicing in the presence of the angels of God
over one sinner who repents" (v. 10).*

Auburn's just not like other college towns. Thank goodness.

Legendary Auburn swimming and diving coach David Marsh captured the essence of what makes Auburn different when he said, "When you do something special at Auburn, the whole town and university celebrate." The occasion for his remark was the 1999 national championship won by the Auburn men's swimming team, their second in three years.

Winning the championship was a real challenge not only because the Tigers were up against 39 teams and 250 athletes but also because the Auburn men had no divers. Ranked number three headed into the championships, the Tigers led after each of first two days of competition, but Stanford was so close everything came down to the final event, the 400 free relay.

Auburn's team of Brock Newman, Brett Hawke, team captain Aaron Ciarla, and Romain Barnier did not fail. They set the water on fire, swimming to new U.S. Open and NCAA records. When Barnier touched the wall, the Tigers were national champions -- again. "This is a dream come true," said NCAA breast-stroke champion Dave Denniston. "That's why I came to Auburn."

The celebration began right there on the pool deck at Indiana University. "I was like a cat on a hot stove," Marsh said. He wasn't

alone as the celebrating continued all the way to Auburn. When the national champions arrived home, Toomer's Corner received its traditional rolling, "causing downtown Auburn to look snow white in April." A coronation ceremony followed, and the champs took the Tiger Walk from the Martin Aquatic Center to the coliseum.

As Marsh pointed out, everybody celebrated.

Auburn just beat Alabama. You got that new job or that promotion. You just held your newborn child in your arms. Life has those grand moments that call for celebration. You may jump up and down and scream in a wild frenzy at Jordan-Hare or share a quiet, sedate candlelight dinner at home -- but you celebrate.

Consider then a celebration that is actually beyond our imagining, one that fills every niche and corner of the very home of God and the angels. Imagine a celebration in Heaven, which also has its grand moments.

They are touched off when someone comes to faith in Jesus. Heaven itself rings with the joyous sounds of the singing and dancing of the celebrating angels. Even God rejoices when just one person – you or someone you have introduced to Christ? -- turns to him.

When you said "yes" to Christ, you made the angels dance.

*When it comes to celebrating, act like you've been there before.*
*-- Terry Bowden*

**God himself joins the angels**
**in heavenly celebration when a single person**
**turns to him through faith in Jesus.**

# CHANGELESS

### Read Hebrews 13:5-16.

*"Jesus Christ is the same yesterday and today and forever" (v. 8).*

**W**hat game is this?

Unhelmeted players let their hair grow long for protection. The V-trick kickoff started the games: Since the rules did not specify a minimum distance for kickoffs, the kicker would touch the ball with his toe, pick it up, and disappear amidst his V-shaped teammates, who then all took off downfield. Spectators rushed onto the field and interfered with the players. The ball was shaped like a watermelon. Referees were anyone from coaches to players to fans who had come simply to watch a game.

This strange, foreign game, "unorganized and mischievous," was college football in its wild and wooly early days, the 1890s and the turn of the century.

A missed season because nobody bothered to schedule any games. A slanted field rather than a level one. A player hiding the ball under a jersey. No scoreboard. A player kicking a field goal by setting the ball on his helmet. No set time for the first and second halves, the length to be determined by agreement of the teams and usually depending upon the weather. Teammates dragging a tackled ball carrier forward.

Largely unregulated and unsophisticated with no forward pass, it was a game we would barely recognize today.

Thank goodness, we might well say. Given the symmetry, the excitement, the passion, and the sheer spectacle that surround today's college game, few, if any, Auburn fans would long for the days when handles were sewn into the uniforms of ball carriers to make them easier to toss.

Football has changed – but then again so has everything else. High definition television and DVDs, cell phones, George Foreman grills, and IMAX theaters may not have even been around when you were sixteen. Think about how style, cars, and tax laws constantly change. Don't be too harsh on the world, though, because you've changed also. You've aged, gained or lost weight, married, changed jobs, or relocated.

Have you ever found yourself bewildered by the rapid pace of change, casting about for something to hold on to that will always be the same, that you can use for an anchor for your life? Is there anything like that in this world?

Sadly, the answer's no. As football illustrates, all the things of this world change.

On the other hand, there's Jesus, who is the same today, the same forever, always dependable, always loving you. You can grab hold of Jesus and never let go.

*Baseball is for the leisurely afternoons of summer and for the unchanging dreams.*
—*Writer Roger Kahn*

**In our ever-changing and bewildering world,
Jesus is the same forever;
his love for you will never change.**

# CROWD CONTROL

**Read Matthew 27:15-26.**

*"When Pilate saw that he could do nothing, but rather that a riot was beginning, he took some water and washed his hands before the crowd" (v. 24 NRSV).*

The Auburn fans booed the decision that turned out to be the difference in the most improbable win in Tiger football history.

On Dec. 2, 1972, second-ranked Alabama led ninth-ranked Auburn 16-0 with 9:15 left to play. When Coach Shug Jordan decided to go for a field goal, some of the Auburn faithful saw it as surrender and booed. Gardner Jett nailed the kick, which, considering the way the game had gone, didn't seem to matter much.

Jordan opted for the kick to put some life into his team. "We went for the field goal to create some enthusiasm," he said. " We had some but we needed more. . . . I remember the crowd booing when we went for the field goal, but those three points turned out to be mighty important."

They did indeed. The stage was set for the most incredible sequence of events in Auburn football history. First, linebacker Bill Newton blocked a Bama punt with 5:30 left and David Langner ran it in from the 25.

Still, Alabama seemed in control by grinding out a pair of first downs and running precious time off the clock. But the Tiger defense held and forced a Crimson Tide punt. The unbelievable

happened when Newton blocked another Alabama punt attempt and Langner scooped it up and scored from the 20 with only 1:34 to play. Auburn won 17-16.

"I didn't know what to think," Langner said about catching Newton's blocked punts. "They just bounced into my hands. All I had to do was pick it up and run. It was by far the greatest thrill I've ever had."

The equally thrilled Auburn crowd certainly wasn't booing any more.

Teenagers seem to catch particular grief about going along with the crowd, but adults, too, often behave in ways contrary to what their conscience tells them is right simply because they fear the disapproval of the people they're with at the time.

So they chuckle at a racial joke. Make fun of a coworker nobody likes. Drink too much and stay out too late. Remain silent when God is cursed. It remains true, though: Just because the crowd does it doesn't make it right. Even Pontius Pilate understood that.

The followers of Jesus Christ are called to separate themselves from the crowd by being disciples. That is, we give to Jesus nothing less than everything we are and everything we have. Jesus is the top priority in a disciple's life, and everything else – everything else – stands behind Jesus. A disciple never goes along with the crowd; he goes along with Jesus.

*Never compromise what you think is right.*

*-- Bear Bryant*

**Just because everybody's doing it doesn't make it right, especially in the way you follow Jesus.**

DAY 38

# PRESSURE POINT

### Read 1 Kings 18:16-40.

*"Answer me, O Lord, answer me, so these people will know that you, O Lord, are God" (v. 37).*

If you can't take the heat, get out of the kitchen.

Jimmy Fibbe once stood in the equivalent of a pizza oven as he withstood withering pressure that would have collapsed a lesser man. Back on Feb. 20, 1960, the perennially powerful Kentucky Wildcats of Adolph Rupp led Auburn 60-59 with five seconds left. Fibbe, a junior who would make All-SEC his senior year, was fouled and faced a one-and-one.

But more than just the game hung in the balance. If he made them both and Auburn won, the Tigers were SEC champions. If he missed, well, it was a great season but not a championship one in an age when only the league champion went on to postseason tournament play.

Auburn's coach was the legendary Joel Eaves, and he had to shout to be heard over the frenzied Auburn crowd that packed Sports Arena. During a time out, Eaves told his players what to do if Fibbe made the first free throw and missed the second one, if he made them both, and if their worst fears were realized and he missed the first one. Fibbe calmly said to Eaves, "Coach, I'm going to make them both." Fibbe said he never forget his coach's reply. Eaves said, "I know you are, but just in case you don't --."

The team benches were on the ends of the court, and Fibbe

had to stand at the free-throw line right in front of the Kentucky bench. With all that pressure on him, he made them both. Auburn won 61-60.

When the game ended, the Auburn students stormed the court and Fibbe found Rupp to shake his hand and to "remind him that he didn't think I was good enough to play there."

You live every day with pressure. As Elijah did so long ago and as Jimmy Fibbe did against Kentucky, you lay it on the line with everybody watching. Your family, coworkers, or employees – they depend on you.

You know the pressure of a deadline, of a job evaluation, of taking the risk of asking someone to go out with you, of driving in rush-hour traffic.

Help in dealing with daily pressure is readily available, and the only price you pay for it is your willingness to believe. God will give you the grace to persevere if you ask prayerfully.

And while you may need some convincing, the pressures of daily living are really small potatoes because they all will pass. The real pressure comes in deciding where you will spend eternity because that decision is forever. You can handle that pressure easily enough by deciding for Jesus. Eternity is then taken care of; the pressure's off – forever.

*Pressure is for tires.*

-- *Charles Barkley*

**The greatest pressure you face in life
concerns where you will spend eternity,
which can be dealt with by deciding for Jesus.**

# DREAM WORLD

**Read Joel 2:26-28.**

*"Your old men will dream dreams, your young men will see visions" (v. 28).*

**P**at Sullivan's childhood dreams came true.

Sullivan, of course, is Auburn's most celebrated quarterback ever, the winner of the 1971 Heisman Trophy as the most outstanding player in college football. His childhood dreams didn't necessarily involve trophies and awards, but they did involve playing football for Auburn.

He was heavily recruited out of John Carroll High in Birmingham, but for Sullivan, Auburn was the only place. He said, "When you're growing up, you're either an Auburn fan or an Alabama fan. I always took sides with Auburn. I thought about other places, but deep down Auburn was where I wanted to go."

The recruiting battle eventually came down to Alabama and Auburn, but in the end Sullivan stayed true to that "deep down" feeling. "It felt right being around Coach Jordan," he said. Part of that came from Jordan's honesty. "He never made outlandish promises that I was going to start and make all-conference," Sullivan recalled. The veteran coach simply told Sullivan he was somebody Auburn really needed in its program and that he would be given every opportunity to play.

His first varsity game was against Wake Forest in 1969. "I was real excited and didn't know what to expect," Sullivan recalled.

# TIGERS

"The band starts playing 'War Eagle,' and you come out from under the stands and it gives you cold chills. You think back to when you were a kid and always wanted to play college football, and now here you are." He overthrew his receiver on his first play, but the students still stood up and cheered.

For Pat Sullivan, dreams did come true.

You have dreams. Maybe to make a lot of money. Write the great American novel. Or have the fairy-tale romance. But dreams often are crushed beneath the weight of everyday living; reality, not dreams, comes to occupy your time, attention, and effort. You've come to understand that achieving your dreams requires a combination of persistence, timing, and providence.

But what if your dreams don't come true because they're not good enough? That is, they're based on the alluring but totally unreliable promises of the world rather than the true promises of God, which are a sure thing.

God calls us to great achievements because God's dreams for us are greater than our dreams for ourselves. Such greatness occurs, though, only when our dreams and God's will for our lives are the same. Your dreams should be worthy of your best – and worthy of God's involvement in making them come true.

*An athlete cannot run with money in his pocket. He must run with*
*hope in his heart and dreams in his head.*
*-- Olympic Gold Medalist Emil Zatopek*

**Dreams based on the world's promises**
**are often crushed; those based on God's promises**
**are a sure thing.**

# TOWEL THROWERS

**Read Numbers 13:25-14:4.**

*"The men who had gone up with him said, 'We can't attack those people; they are stronger than we are'" (v. 13:31).*

**A**n unknown night supervisor at the Opelika bus station is one of the Auburn football program's greatest benefactors.

How could that be? Probably unknowingly, he played a hand in preventing a freshman named Bo Jackson from quitting football and dropping out of Auburn. Jackson, of course, is legend. He won the Heisman Trophy in 1985, and in 2007 ESPN named him the eighth greatest player in college football history. He was a three-time All-SEC selection and a two-time All-America. He set an SEC record by averaging 6.6 yards per carry in his career. In 1992, his number 34 was officially retired at Auburn, joining Pat Sullivan's number 7 and the number 88 of Sullivan's favorite receiver, Terry Beasley.

But the week before the Alabama game in 1982 the man many believe to be the greatest athlete in Auburn history went down to the Greyhound bus station on Tenth Street in Opelika to go home, to quit. Bo had come to buy a ticket for Birmingham, but he sat alone in a corner of the station for eight hours while the buses came and went. He was simply a lonely and confused young man, trying to figure things out. "I was depressed, disillusioned with a lot of things," Jackson said. "I didn't think I could keep on

handling all the pressure that had been put on me."

Finally, around 2 a.m., the night supervisor walked over to the strong-looking figure in the corner of the bus station and told him he couldn't loiter in the bus station any longer: He had to buy a ticket or leave. Bo left. He hitched a ride back to the dorm and put aside forever any thoughts of quitting.

And the next week, Bo carved his name in Auburn lore when he went over the top to beat Alabama 23-22. The rest, as they say, is history.

Remember that time you quit a high-school sports team? Bailed out of a relationship? Walked away from that job with the goals unachieved? Sometimes quitting is the most sensible way to minimize your losses, so you may well at times in your life give up on something or someone.

In your relationship with God, however, you should remember the people of Israel, who quit when the Promised Land was theirs for the taking. They forgot one fact of life you never should: God never gives up on you. That means you should never, ever give up on God. No matter how tired or discouraged you get, no matter that it seems your prayers aren't getting through to God, no matter what – quitting on God is not an option. He is preparing a blessing for you, and in his time, he will bring it to fruition -- if you don't quit on him.

*Once you learn to quit, it becomes a habit.*

*– Vince Lombardi*

**Whatever else you give up on in your life, don't give up on God; he will never ever give up on you.**

# CONFIDENCE MAN

**Read Micah 7:5-7.**

*"As for me, I will look to the Lord, I will wait for the God of my salvation" (v. 7 NRSV).*

**Z**eke Smith was such a confident ball player that in a crucial game in the 1957 drive to the national championship, he promised he would get the ball for Auburn -- and then promptly caused and recovered a fumble on the next play.

The 1957 Tigers lived by their defense, which may have been the best in school history. They gave up only 28 points in the ten games of the regular season; no SEC team scored on Auburn's defense; nobody scored on the first-team defense all season. One of the four touchdowns scored on Auburn was on an interception return.

Smith came to Auburn as a fullback, but the coaches quickly moved him to the line, which was fine with Smith; he just wanted to play -- and play he did. He was twice All-America, and he won the Outland Trophy in 1958 as the nation's best interior lineman.

His confidence played a key role in his success, and nowhere was that more evident than in the Georgia game of 1957. Auburn was 7-0 and ranked number three. With the team's reliance on its defense, it was a frightening moment when quarterback Lloyd Nix -- who never lost a game at Auburn as a starting quarterback -- pitched the ball behind halfback Tommy Lorino. Lorino slipped on the wet grass trying to get back to the ball, and the Bulldogs

recovered inside the Auburn 20.

Smith simply gave his quarterback a pat on the backside and a big smile. "Don't worry, Lloyd," he said. "I'll get it back." "Sure enough," Nix said, "he made the guy fumble on the next play and recovered the fumble." Auburn went on to win 6-0.

Zeke Smith was one confident football player.

You need confidence in all areas of your life. You're confident the company you work for will pay you on time, or you wouldn't go to work. You turn the ignition confident your car will start. When you flip a switch, you expect the light to come on.

Confidence in other people and in things is often misplaced, though. Companies go broke; car batteries die; light bulbs burn out. Even the people you love the most sometimes let you down.

So where can you place your trust with absolute confidence you won't be betrayed? In the promises of God.

Such confidence is easy, of course, when everything's going your way, but what about when you cry as Micah did, "What misery is mine!" As Micah declares, that's when your confidence in God must be its strongest. That's when you wait for the Lord confident that God will not fail you, that he will never let you down.

*When it gets right down to the wood-chopping, the key to winning is confidence.*

-- *Former College Football Coach Darrell Royal*

**People, things, and organizations will
let you down; only God can be trusted
absolutely and confidently.**

DAY 42

# GOOD LUCK

### Read 1 Samuel 28:3-20.

*"Saul then said to his attendants, 'Find me a woman who is a medium, so I may go and inquire of her'" (v. 7).*

Stan White played at Auburn with a four-leaf clover attached to his ankle.

White is the most prolific passer in Auburn history with 8,016 career passing yards; he is also the school's career offensive leader. In 1993 the Birmingham Monday Morning Quarterback Club named him the SEC's Most Valuable Back. During that sensational 1993 season, White played wearing a traditional good-luck sign. But he's not superstitious; it was an act of love.

What White wore was a four-leaf clover, a gift from a 9-year-old whose birthday was the same as his. An avid Auburn fan who was already into poring over the media guide, she wrote White a letter in 1990 when he was a freshman, and a friendship grew. She found the four-leaf clover in 1992 the week before the Georgia game of White's junior year and sent it to him with a note that said, "This is my best good luck charm in the world." White had his greatest game ever, and after that he wore the clover in his sock.

His senior year against Georgia he lost his symbol of affection that doubled as a good-luck charm. "The first play of the game, I got hit, my socks got swiped down and I lost it," he said. "At the end of that series, I got a marker and drew a four-leaf clover on my

tape." He asked his fan to find another, but this was November and she couldn't. He drew one on his tape again and eventually had a four-leaf clover tattooed on his ankle in honor of his little friend's gift.

Four-leaf clover and all, White quarterbacked the Tigers to a perfect 11-0 record in 1993 under new head coach Terry Bowden.

Black cats are right pretty. A medium is a steak. A key chain with a rabbit's foot wasn't too lucky for the rabbit. And what in the world is a blarney stone? About as superstitious as you get is to say "God bless you" when somebody sneezes.

You look indulgently upon good-luck charms, tarot cards, astrology, palm readers, and the like; they're amusing and harmless. What's the problem? Nothing as long as you conduct yourself with the belief that superstitious objects and rituals – from broken mirrors to your daily horoscope – can't effect good or bad luck. You aren't willing to let such notions and nonsense rule your life.

The danger of superstition lies in its ability to lure you into trusting it, thus allowing it some degree of influence over your life. In that case, it subverts God's rightful place.

Whether or not it's superstition, something does rule your life. It should be God – and God alone.

*I don't believe in a jinx or a hex. Winning depends on how well you block and tackle.*

*-- Shug Jordan*

**Superstition may not rule your life, but
something does; it should be God and God alone.**

# STAR POWER

**Read Luke 10:1-3, 17-20.**

*"The Lord appointed seventy-two others and sent them two by two ahead of him to every town and place where he was about to go" (v. 1).*

**Y**ou would think a team that completely overwhelms the field in the NCAA swimming championships would be led by a star, a media darling who splashed his way to a whole bunch of points. In the case of the 2003 Auburn men's swimming team, you would be wrong.

That team churned through the water to one of the greatest and most complete victories in NCAA swimming history. In Austin, Texas, in March, the Auburn men won the third national title in program history (and joined the women's squad as national champions) by leaving the field sputtering in their wake.

They became only the second team in NCAA history to tally more than 600 points (609.5), and they won by an incredible 196.5 points, Texas finishing a distant second with 413 points and Stanford an invisible third with 374 points. The competition was essentially over after the first day when the Tigers climbed out of the pool with a commanding 85-point lead.

And they did it without a star. Instead, they did something really remarkable and rare: All nineteen athletes on the NCAA roster contributed points to the win. Equally as impressive, the Tigers scored points in all 21 events.

# TIGERS

When the celebrating was over, Coach David Marsh chose to call attention to his team's lack of star power. "The fact that all 19 athletes scored in every event shows the diversity of this team," he said. "We are not about one star. I am just delighted." These no-name non-stars made All-America — 61 times.

Sports teams are like other organizations in that they may have a star but the star would be nothing without the supporting cast. It's the same in a private company, in a government bureaucracy, in a military unit, and just about any other team of people with a common goal.

That includes the team known as a church. It may have its "star" in the preacher, who is – like the quarterback or the company CEO – the most visible representative of the team. Preachers are, after all, God's paid, trained professionals.

But when Jesus assembled a team of seventy-two folks, he didn't have anybody on the payroll or any seminary graduates. All he had were no-names who loved him. And nothing has changed. God's church still depends on those whose only pay is the satisfaction of serving and whose only qualification is their love for God.

God's church needs you.

*You may have the greatest bunch of individual stars in the world, but if they don't play together, the club won't be worth a dime.*
*– Babe Ruth*

**Yes, the church needs its professional clergy,
but it also needs those who serve as volunteers
because they love God; the church needs you.**

# HOMELESS

**Read Matthew 8:18-22.**

*"Jesus replied, 'Foxes have holes and birds of the air have nests, but the Son of Man has no place to lay his head'"* (v. 20).

Auburn's football schedule features a mess of home games every year, but for much of their football history, the Tigers were, in effect, homeless.

In the early days of their football history, the Tigers played only a few games in the Loveliest Village. They consistently hit the road to take advantage of larger crowds, bigger gates, and more money. All four of the games in 1892, Auburn's first football season, were played in Atlanta. In 1893, the Tigers played their first-ever in-state games -- at Montgomery and Birmingham. Not until 1896 — the fifth season of Auburn football -- did the Tigers have a home game, a 45-0 ripping of Georgia Tech.

Even after the schedule was expanded to ten games, the Tigers rarely played at home. The Orange-Bowl champions of 1937 went 6-3-2 and did not play a single game in Auburn. They rode the rails to New Orleans, Philadelphia, Houston, Baton Rouge, and several less exotic locations.

The construction of Auburn Stadium didn't curtail the Tigers' travels either. The first game played in what is now Jordan-Hare was on Nov. 30, 1939, a 7-7 tie with Florida. This was Auburn's 48th season of football. In 1940 and again in 1942, though, Auburn

still played only one game at home, against Clemson both years. Then from 1946 through 1949, Auburn played only one game at home each season. Not until 1950 did the Tigers have as many as three home games. Not until 1960, the Tigers' 69th year of football and Shug Jordan's tenth year as head coach, did they play half of their ten-game schedule in Auburn.

For decades, the Tigers may as well not have had a home field so rarely did they play there.

Rock bottom in America has a face: the bag lady pushing a shopping cart; the scruffy guy with a beard and a backpack at the interstate exit holding a cardboard sign. Look closer at that bag lady or that scruffy guy, though, and you may see desperate women with children fleeing violence, veterans haunted by their combat experiences, or sick or injured workers.

Few of us are indifferent to the homeless when we're around them. They often raise quite strong passions, whether we regard them as a ministry or a nuisance. They trouble us, perhaps because we realize that we're only one catastrophic illness and a few paychecks away from joining them. They remind us, therefore, of how tenuous our hold upon material success really is.

But they also stir our compassion because we serve a Lord who – like them -- had no home, and for whom, the homeless, too, are his children.

*Some people beat up on the homeless for sport.*
*-- Maryland State Sen. Lisa Gladden.*

**Because they, too, are God's children,**
**the homeless merit our compassion, not our scorn.**

# FEAR FACTOR

**Read Matthew 14:22-33.**

*"[The disciples] cried out in fear. But Jesus immediately said to them: 'Take courage! It is I. Don't be afraid'" (vv. 26-27).*

**H**enry Harris was fearless. Pioneers have to be.

"I'd go in [a] restaurant and get some hamburgers and bring them out. We'd sit in the car and talk, and we'd take some hamburgers back to his family." So did Auburn assistant coach Rudy Davalos describe his recruiting of Harris. Why would they eat burgers in the car? Harris couldn't go inside the restaurant. This was 1968, and Harris was black.

He grew up in Boligee, Ala., living with his mother and four siblings in an abandoned service station. His mother was a widow who held the family together as a lunchroom helper. For Harris, basketball was his ticket out.

Most folks assumed he would head north or west to play college ball because neither Auburn nor Alabama had a black athlete. Villanova, for instance, recruited him hard, the coach asking Harris, "Why in the world would [you] want to go to Auburn?"

On March 14, 1968, though, Harris made history by signing a scholarship to play basketball for Auburn. His signature made him Auburn's only African-American athlete until football player James Owens arrived a year later.

He thus became "a pioneer in changing and frightening times."

Harris wasn't frightened, though. Davalos said of him, "He seemed to not be afraid of things. He was such a likeable guy."

Everything didn't turn out as planned for this fearless pioneer. He didn't really become a star at Auburn, earning third-team All-SEC honors as a senior. After being drafted in the eighth round by the Houston Rockets, Harris was cut before the season began and never played a game in the pros. Harris' courage, though, opened doors for others and changed sports at Auburn forever.

Some fears are universal; others are particular. Speaking to a group may require a heavy dose of antiperspirant. Elevator walls may feel as though they're closing in on you. And don't even get started on being in the dark with spiders and snakes during a thunderstorm.

We all live in fear, and God knows this. Dozens of passages in the Bible urge us not to be afraid. God isn't telling us to lose our wariness of oncoming cars or big dogs with nasty dispositions; this is a helpful fear God instilled in us for protection.

What God does wish driven from our lives is a spirit of fear that dominates us, that makes our lives miserable and keeps us from doing what we should, such as sharing our faith. In commanding that we not be afraid, God reminds us that when we trust completely in him, we find peace that calms our fears.

*Let me win. But if I cannot win, let me be brave in the attempt.*
— *Special Olympics Motto*

**You have your own peculiar set of fears,
but they should never paralyze you
because God is greater than anything you fear.**

DAY 46

# AMERICAN HERO

### Read 1 Samuel 16:1-13.

*"Do not consider his appearance or his height, for . . . the*
*Lord does not look at the things man looks at. . . . The*
*Lord looks at the heart" (v. 7).*

**K**irk Newell was a great football player. But more than that, he was a true American hero.

Newell was the left halfback on the 1913 Auburn team that went 8-0-0 and launched a streak of 23 games without a loss. The first Tiger team to win eight games, the 1913 team was challenged only by LSU 7-0 and Vanderbilt 13-7. With a defense that gave up only thirteen points all season, the Tigers were the Southern Conference champions. Newell was named All-Southern, as were end Robbie Robinson, fullback Red Harris, and tackle Frank Lockwood.

Daniel Gibson, who played with Newell, felt that Newell was cheated of the national recognition he should have received because of the media's bias against Southern football. "Kirk Newell would have been all-American if we had been known in the world, but they just knew Harvard and Yale and so on," Gibson said. "He was one of the greatest halfbacks I ever saw. He'd go down the field telling his blockers, 'Block him to the left, block him to the right.'"

But Newell's greatness did not end after his playing days at Auburn were over. During World War I in a trench in France, Lt.

# TIGERS

Newell threw himself on a hand grenade to save his men. He was injured, his life saved only because a canteen shielded him from some of the force of the explosion. He was decorated for heroism, surviving to die an old man in 1967. Newell's daughter recalled, "The hand grenade got lost in the leaves. But he knew it was there and he tried to save the others." She kept the canteen "with that terrible hole in it."

Kirk Newell was a true American hero.

A hero is commonly thought of as someone who performs brave and dangerous feats that save or protect someone's life – as Kirk Newell did during World War I. You figure that excludes you.

But ask your son about that when you show him how to bait a hook, or your daughter when you show up for her dance recital. Look into the eyes of those Little Leaguers you help coach.

Ask God about heroism when you're steady in your faith. For God, a hero is a person with the heart of a servant. And if a hero is a servant who acts to save other's lives, then the greatest hero of all is Jesus Christ.

God seeks heroes today, those who will proclaim the name of their hero – Jesus – proudly and boldly, no matter how others may scoff or ridicule. God knows a hero when he sees him -- by what's in his heart.

*Heroes and cowards feel exactly the same fear; heroes just act differently.*
*-- Boxing trainer Cus D'Amato*

**God's heroes are those who remain steady**
**in their faith while serving others.**

# ONE TOUGH COOKIE

### Read 2 Corinthians 11:21b-29.

*"Besides everything else, I face daily the pressure of my concern for all the churches" (v. 28).*

**R**unning back Wallace Clark was one tough football player. Just ask Pat Sullivan.

Clark, who was taken by the Atlanta Falcons in the 1971 NFL draft, scored the winning touchdown in one of Auburn's greatest comeback victories over Alabama. In 1970, the fans were barely in their seats before Alabama led 17-0. But Sullivan and Terry Beasley led a stirring comeback, capped by Clark's three-yard run with less than four minutes to play that gave Auburn a 33-28 win.

Sullivan once called Clark "the toughest guy who ever walked." To back up his claim, he told of what he said was "probably the finest example of toughness I've ever seen." In a game against Georgia, Sullivan hit Clark with what was supposed to be a routine screen pass. Clark was promptly hit so hard by a Bulldog defender that his helmet was knocked off. Undeterred and helmetless, Clark continued to run until he was hit in the face by a helmet when he was tackled.

Sullivan said, "It split his lip away from his gum. They put gauze in his mouth, and he came back and played the rest of the game. He'd come back to the huddle and take the gauze out and spit out a mouthful of blood." Sullivan was doubly impressed

because Wallace didn't have to play; the team had backups. He was just determined to play. "He had worked all week in practice, and he was going to play in the game," Sullivan said, "After the game, he had about 15 stitches."

Wallace Clark was one tough cookie.

You don't have to be an Auburn running back to be tough. In America today, toughness isn't restricted to physical accomplishments and brute strength. Going to work every morning even when you feel bad, sticking by your rules for your children in a society that ridicules parental authority, making hard decisions about your aging parents' care often over their objections — you've got to be tough every day just to live honorably, decently, and justly.

Living faithfully requires toughness, too, though in America chances are you won't be imprisoned, stoned, or flogged this week for your faith as Paul was. Still, contemporary society exerts subtle, psychological, daily pressures on you to turn your back on your faith and your values. Popular culture promotes promiscuity, atheism, and gutter language; your children's schools have kicked God out; the corporate culture advocates amorality before the shrine of the almighty dollar.

You have to hang tough to keep the faith.

*Tough times don't last but tough people do.*
*— Former NBA player A.C. Green*

**Life demands more than mere physical toughness;**
**you must be spiritually tough too.**

# OUT WITH THE OLD

**Read Hebrews 8:3-13.**

*"The ministry Jesus has received is as superior to theirs as the covenant of which he is mediator is superior to the old one, and it is founded on better promises" (v. 6).*

The most successful men's sports program in Auburn's history doesn't even exist anymore.

Imagine losing to only one SEC opponent in 28 years. That's impossible! And yet that's what the Auburn men's wrestling team did under legendary coach Arnold "Swede" Umbach. Umbach came to Auburn in 1944 as an assistant football coach, and he launched the Auburn wrestling program in 1946. When he retired in 1973, his teams had won 25 Southern Intercollegiate Wrestling Association championships, had a record in dual meets of 249-28-5, and, yes, had lost only once to an SEC opponent. Umbach was a tough taskmaster, "but his wrestlers loved him like a father. He taught lessons in competing and lessons in living."

Sonny Dragoin, who wrestled for Auburn and served for 23 years as coach of the Auburn men's golf team, said of Umbach, "Without a doubt, he was the best wrestling coach in the United States. He didn't have any scholarships and didn't need them. He was an outstanding teacher of the sport and beyond reproach as a person. I would have trusted him with my life."

Umbach is a member of both the National Wrestling Hall of Fame and the Alabama Sports Hall of Fame.

# TIGERS

But that's all part of ancient history now. The program was discontinued in 1981, and Umbach died in 1993. Wrestling at Auburn is long gone, largely forgotten by today's students, the championship trophies merely museum curiosity pieces. The wrestling program was rendered obsolete, the victim of new emphases in college sports.

Your car's running fine, but the miles are adding up. Time for a trade-in. Your TV's still delivering a sharp picture, but those HDTV's are awesome. So are those newer, faster computers. And how about those lawn mowers that turn on a dime?

Out with the old, in with the new — we're always looking for the newest thing on the market. In our faith life, that means the new covenant God gave us through Jesus Christ. An old covenant did exist, one based on the law God struck with the Hebrew people. But God used this old covenant as the basis to go one better and establish a covenant available to the whole world. This new way is a covenant of grace between God and anyone who lives a life of faith in Jesus.

Don't get caught waiting for a newer, improved covenant, though; the promises God gave us through Jesus couldn't get any better.

*The old ballplayer cared about the name on the front [of the jersey]. The new ballplayer cares about the name on the back.*
*— Former major leaguer Steve Garvey*

**No matter how old it is,**
**it just doesn't get any better**
**than God's new covenant through Jesus Christ.**

DAY 49

# THE SUB

### Read Galatians 3:10-14.

*"Christ redeemed us from the curse of the law by becoming a curse for us" (v. 13).*

The most dramatic hit in the history of Auburn baseball was delivered by a substitute playing because the starter was injured.

On May 24, 1997, the Tigers played Florida State in the East Regional with a trip to the College World Series on the line. Auburn trailed 7-5 when with two outs in the bottom of the ninth, Tim Hudson walked, and Derek Reif legged out an infield hit.

That left the fate of the Tigers in the hands of sophomore catcher David Ross, who was in the lineup only because starter Casey Dunn had broken a hand in the regional opener. Ross was a .230 hitter who had played sparingly, and he looked it with two feeble swings that put him in an 0-2 hole.

He then managed a foul tip. At first it seemed the Seminole catcher had held on; some of the FSU players even started running onto the field. But the ball hit the ground. Coach Hal Baird remarkably and calmly told his players in the dugout, "When he hits it out, don't get in his way. He has to touch all the bases."

The next pitch was outside, and then Ross did the unbelievable: He slammed a high pitch that sailed deep into leftfield. The FSU leftfielder -- a future Atlanta Brave named Matt Diaz -- raced for the fence, stopped, and dropped his head. Ross had hit a home run for an 8-7 Tiger win.

# TIGERS

Baird tried to keep his ecstatic players off the field and was knocked face first into the dirt for his troubles. One of Auburn's greatest icons, Billy Hitchcock, said he considered Ross' homer one of the top two or three moments in Auburn athletic history. It left Auburn fans from all over screaming, dancing, and crying and the FSU faithful sitting in stunned silence. And the blow was delivered by a sub.

Wouldn't it be cool if you had a substitute like David Ross for all life's hard stuff? Telling of a death in the family? Call in your sub. Breaking up with your boyfriend? Job interview? Chemistry test? Crucial presentation at work? Let the sub handle it.

We do have such a substitute, but not for the matters of life. Instead, Jesus is our substitute for matters of life and death. Since Jesus has already made it, we don't have to make the sacrifice God demands for forgiveness and salvation.

One of the ironies of our age is that many people desperately grope for a substitute for Jesus. Mysticism, human philosophies such as Scientology, false religions such as Hinduism and Islam, cults, New Age approaches that preach happiness without responsibility or accountability – they and others like them are all pitiful, inadequate substitutes for Jesus.

Accept no substitutes. It's Jesus or nothing.

*I never substitute just to substitute. The only way a guy gets off the floor is if he dies.*
— *Former basketball coach Abe Lemons*

**There is no substitute for Jesus,**
**the consummate substitute.**

# CLOCKWORK

**Read Matthew 25:1-13.**

*"Keep watch, because you do not know the day or the hour" (v. 13).*

The scoreboard clock lied. And it may have cost Auburn an undefeated season.

The Tigers of 1963 went 9-1, the lone blemish a 13-10 upset at the hands of Mississippi State. They were 6-0 with wins over Houston, Tennessee, Kentucky, Chattanooga, Georgia Tech, and Florida and were ranked fifth in the nation when they rolled into Jackson on Nov. 9.

Quarterback Jimmy Sidle -- an All-America that season -- ran for a 47-yard touchdown to stake Auburn to an early 7-3 lead. Then, late in the first half, Sidle had another 47-yard play, this one a pass to end Howard Simpson that carried to the Bulldog 13.

That's when the clock lied. The scoreboard appeared to show only six seconds left in the half. The Tigers had time outs, but Coach Shug Jordan made what seemed like the correct decision by sending kicker Woody Woodall in. He booted a 30-yard field goal for a 10-3 Auburn lead.

Only then did the Tigers realize the scoreboard lights were malfunctioning, and that 46 seconds had been left in the half when Woodall made his field goal. That would have been plenty of time for Auburn to run a couple of plays and possibly score a touchdown.

The failure to score that touchdown turned out to be crucial. State kicked a 36-yard field goal with 22 seconds left to win 14-13. That kick would have done them no good had Auburn been leading 14-3 at halftime, instead of 10-3, and 17-11 late in the game, instead of 13-11.

With time on their side, the Tigers went on to beat Georgia, FSU, and Alabama, the latter a 10-8 defensive thriller at Legion Field. They finished the season ranked fifth in the nation and went to the Orange Bowl, Jordan's first major bowl.

We may pride ourselves on our time management, but the truth is that we don't manage time; it manages us. Hurried and harried, we live by schedules that seem to have too much what and too little when. By setting the bedside alarm at night, we even let the clock determine how much down time we get. A life of leisure actually means one in which time is of no importance.

Every second of our life – all the time we have – is a gift from God, who dreamed up time in the first place. We would do well, therefore, to consider what God considers to be good time management. After all, Jesus himself warned us against mismanaging the time we have. From God's point of view, using our time wisely means being prepared at every moment for Jesus' return, which will occur -- well, only time will tell when.

*We didn't lose the game; we just ran out of time.*
— *Vince Lombardi*

**We mismanage our time
when we fail to prepare for Jesus' return
even though we don't know when that will be.**

# A BETTER PLACE

**Read Hebrews 11:13-16.**

*"They were longing for a better country — a heavenly one" (v. 16a).*

When Kyle Davis shot free throws, people noticed.

Davis is the greatest shot-blocker in Auburn basketball history. He completed his career on the Plains after the 2003-04 season with 360 blocks, the Auburn school record and the second most in SEC history.

Tiger fans naturally whooped it up and high-fived every time Davis sent an opponent's shot back to where it came from, but his trips to the free-throw line beginning in his junior season also drew notice. That's because after Feb. 7, 2003, every time Davis stepped to the line, he pointed up. Many players have unusual routines that help them make free throws, but Davis' unique action had nothing to do with basketball. Rather, it was a reminder and a tribute.

On Feb. 7, 2003, Davis' mother died of cancer; she was only 43. So when he went to the line and pointed toward Heaven, "I do that to let her know that every point I make, every basket I score, is for her," he explained.

His mother was the reason Davis was able to achieve what he did during the 2003-04 season. "I just kept going out there and knowing that she would want me to keep playing and not sit there and be sad," Davis said.

But there was something more that kept Davis going after his mother's untimely death. Marco Killingsworth admired how Davis persevered despite his heart-wrenching loss, but Killingsworth also had insight into what helped his teammate make it through this tough time. "He was more positive about [his mother's death], knowing his mom was in a better place," Killingsworth said.

America is a nation of nomads, packing up the U-Haul and the car and moving on the average about once every five years. We move because we're always seeking something better. Better schools for the kids. A job with better career opportunities. Better weather.

We're seeking that better place that will make our lives better. Quite often, though, we wind up in a place or in circumstances that are just different, not better. So we try again.

God is very aware of this deep longing in our hearts for something better than what we have now. As only he can, he has made provision for it. What God has prepared for us, however, isn't a place that's just better, but rather a place that is perfect. He has also thoughtfully provided clear directions about how to get there, though we won't get any help from our GPS.

Jesus is the way to that place, that perfect place called Heaven.

*When you play a sport, you have two things in mind. One is to get into the Hall of Fame and the other is to go to Heaven when you die.*
*-- Golfer Lee Trevino*

**God knows our deep longing for a better place,**
**so he has prepared one for us: Heaven.**

# SEEING THE VISION

**Read Acts 26:1, 9-23.**

*"So then, . . . I was not disobedient to the vision from heaven" (v. 19).*

**C**raig Stevens saw it coming.

An upset of West Virginia was on the line on Sept. 19, 2009, when first-year Tiger head coach Gene Chizik called a time out to check on his defense. Auburn led by four with less than four minutes to play, but the Mountaineers' potent offense had the ball. "I want[ed] to see a guy's eyes and see what's in him," Chizik explained.

Chizik's desire to get up close with his defense was certainly understandable. The game had been "a nightmare" for the defense, which gave up more than 500 yards. When it came to junior linebacker Craig Stevens, however, Chizik needn't have bothered to check. Stevens, who would be named the SEC Defensive Player of the Week, was already dreaming of the play he was about to make, one that he saw coming.

West Virginia had gashed Auburn all night long with screen passes, consistently taking advantage of the aggressive Tiger defense. Stevens and a couple of teammates used the time out to share their conviction that another screen was coming. "We had a feeling," Stevens said.

His vision came true when he blitzed on the first play and nobody blocked him. "I knew it was coming," Stevens said. So he

stopped his rush and sure enough, the pass came. He tipped the ball, grabbed it, and rambled 15 yards for a touchdown that put the final tally of 40-31 on the scoreboard with 3:41 left.

"It happened so fast, I didn't believe it at first," Stevens said. But it was true. He had his first career interception and his first collegiate touchdown -- just as he had envisioned it on the sideline before the play began.

To speak of visions is often to risk their being lumped with palm readings, Ouija boards, seances, horoscopes, and other such useless mumbo-jumbo. The danger such mild amusements pose, however, is very real in that they indicate a reliance on something other than God. It is God who knows the future; it is God who has a vision and a plan for your life; it is God who has the answers you seek as you struggle to find your way.

You probably do have a vision for your life, a plan for how it should unfold. It's the dream you pursue through your family, your job, your hobbies, your interests. But your vision inspires a fruitful life only if it is compatible with God's plan. As the apostle Paul found out, you ignore God's vision at your peril. But if you pursue it, you'll find an even more glorious life than you could ever have envisioned for yourself.

*If I could see into the future, I wouldn't be sitting here talking to you doorknobs. I'd be out investing in the stock market.*
*-- Boston Celtic Kevin McHale to reporters*

**Your grandest vision for the future**
**pales beside the vision God has of**
**what the two of you can accomplish together.**

# FUTURE PERFECT

### Read Matthew 6:25-34.

*"Do not worry about tomorrow, for tomorrow will worry about itself" (v. 34).*

Even as they practiced, the members of the Auburn men's basketball team of 1984-85 "wondered what their futures held." They didn't know that they were about to take the program to a place it had never been before.

As the SEC basketball tournament neared, Auburn men's basketball was in disarray. Midway through the season, Sonny Smith resigned as head coach. The Tigers finished 8-10 in the SEC and were seeded eighth in the SEC tournament, which meant they had to win four games in four days, which had never been done. "Not even Auburn players held out hope of winning the tournament." "We didn't know what was going on," freshman center Jeff Moore said.

The Tigers whipped Ole Miss 68-60 and then raised a few eyebrows with a 58-55 upset of regular-season champion LSU. When they stunned Florida 43-42, the Tigers were in the finals against Alabama, which had beaten them twice in the regular season. In one of Auburn's greatest games ever, the Tigers won 53-49 in overtime.

But the surprising SEC champions weren't through. Seeded tenth in the East Region of the NCAA Tournament, they stunned Purdue 59-58 behind 20 points from Chuck Person and 19 from

freshman Chris Morris. The Tigers then pulled another upset, toppling mighty Kansas 66-64. Frank Ford scored 23 points and Person added 21.

Auburn was in the Sweet 16 for the first time in school history. The run ended with a six-point loss to North Carolina, but the 22-12 Tigers of 1984-85 had turned an uncertain future into a present glory.

We worry about many things, but nothing tops the frequency with which we fret about tomorrow. How would we live if I lost my job? How can we pay for our children's college? What will I do when my parents can't take care of themselves? What will the Tigers do next season?

Amid our worries about the future, along comes Jesus to tell us, in effect, "Don't worry. Be happy." Well, that's all right for Jesus, but he never had a mortgage to pay or had to suffer teenagers in the house.

In telling us how to approach tomorrow, though, Jesus understood a crucial aspect of the future: Your future is determined by how you live in the present. Particularly is this true in your spiritual life. God has carefully planned your eternal future to include unremitting glory, joy, and peace. It's called Heaven.

You must, however, claim that future in the present through faith in Jesus. And then – don't worry about it.

*The future ain't what it used to be.*

-- *Yogi Berra*

**You lay claim to a sure future**
**through a present faith in Jesus Christ.**

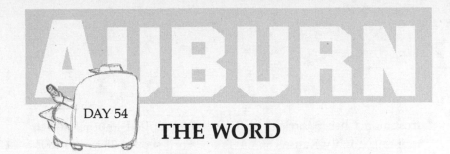

# THE WORD

## Read Matthew 12:33-37.

*"For out of the overflow of the heart the mouth speaks.
The good man brings good things out of the good stored
up in him, and the evil man brings evil things out of the
evil stored up in him" (vv. 34b-35).*

Terry Henley always had something to say – even about Bear
Bryant.

Henley "was a trash talker before trash talking was cool. . . .
Henley talked on the field, off the field, in the locker room. He
was a non-stop one-liner."

Before the Alabama game in 1972, Bryant denigrated Auburn
as a "cow college" which he'd rather beat once than Texas ten
times in the Cotton Bowl. Henley was ready, declaring, "That's
pretty ill-mannered for a grown man who hasn't won the game
yet. We are going to send him back to plowing."

Henley's boast stood up, and after the 17-16 "Punt, Bama, Punt"
win, he couldn't pass up the chance to rub it in: "We took 'em like
a capsule. Chattanooga hit us harder than they did."

Henley was much more than talk. During that sensational
10-1 1972 season, he led Auburn in rushing with 843 yards. That
was good enough to lead the league in rushing yards per game.
Remarkably, he did not fumble the entire season; he was named
the SEC's top running back. In 2000 he was inducted into the
Alabama Sports Hall of Fame.

He gained all those yards despite defenses aligned to stop him and a tendency that annoyed players on both sides of the line. Offensive lineman Mac Lorendo said Henley would "tell those big defensive linemen where we were going to run the ball and crow about how they couldn't stop him. He had everybody wanting to kill him — them and us."

Terry Henley always liked to have the last word.

These days, everybody's got something to say and likely as not a place to say it. Talk radio, 24-hour sports and news TV channels, *The View*. Talk has really become cheap.

But words still have power, and that includes not just those of the talking heads, hucksters, and pundits on television, but yours also. Your words are perhaps the most powerful force you possess for good or for bad. The words you speak today can belittle, wound, humiliate, and destroy. They can also inspire, heal, protect, and create. Your words both shape and define you. They also reveal to the world the depth of your faith.

Don't ever make the mistake of underestimating the power of the spoken word. After all, speaking the Word was the only means Jesus had to get his message across – and look what he managed to do.

Watch what you say because others sure will.

*You can motivate players better with kind words than you can with a whip.*
*– Legendary college football coach Bud Wilkinson*

**Choose your words carefully; they are the most powerful force you have for good or for bad.**

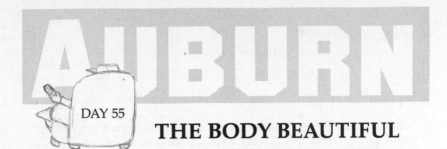

# THE BODY BEAUTIFUL

### Read 1 Corinthians 6:12-20.

*"Do you not know that your body is a temple of the Holy
Spirit, who is in you, whom you have received from God?
... Honor God with your body" (vv. 19, 20b).*

It's a field of dreams.

Auburn fans naturally would say that about Plainsman Park,
home of the Auburn baseball Tigers, claiming unashamedly
that it's the best collegiate stadium in the country. Well, they're
right; it is. Prior to the 2003 season, a *Baseball America* poll picked
Plainsman Park as the best college ballpark in the country.

The park hosted its first SEC baseball in 1950 and seats slightly
more than 4,000 fans. A massive $4.2 million facelift in the 1990s
transformed the field into "a renaissance of Camden Yard proportions."

The obvious beauty and uniqueness of the park, which has the
look and feel of old-time parks and includes its own versions of
the brick backstop of Chicago's Wrigley Field and the legendary
"Green Monster" of Boston's Fenway Park, isn't all that that lures
top talent to Auburn. The baseball facility includes not only
Plainsman Park but the Strength and Rehabilitation Center,
completed in 2004. The players' clubhouse features among its
amenities an indoor hitting tunnel and a team lounge area.

The intimate park is a fan's delight also. Seats down Plainsman's foul lines are close to the field. Front-row box seats are only

four feet off the ground and 40 feet from the first- and third-base bags, and the backstop is only 60 feet from home plate. There's even a terraced lawn down the left field line.

It's a fact: There's not a better place in the country to watch a college baseball game than Plainsman Park. The Tigers and their fans do deserve the best, don't they?

While you may feel that you, too, deserve only the best when it comes to your personal playing field, you may not see a field of dreams when you look into a mirror. Too heavy, too short, too pale, too gray — there's always something wrong because we compare ourselves to an impossible standard Hollywood and fashion magazines have created, and we are inevitably disappointed.

God must have been quite partial to your body, though, because he personally fashioned it and gave it to you free of charge. Your body, like everything else in your life, is thus a gift from God. But God didn't stop there. He then quite voluntarily chose to inhabit your body, sharing it with you in the person of the Holy Spirit.

What an act of consummate ungratefulness it is then to abuse your God-given body by violating God's standards for living. To do so is in fact to dishonor God.

*If you don't do what's best for your body, you're the one who comes up on the short end.*

*-- Julius Erving*

**You may not have a fine opinion of your body,
but God thought enough of it
to personally create it for you.**

DAY 56

# NO GETTING OVER IT

### Read Ephesians 2:1-10.

*"It is by grace you have been saved, through faith -- and this not from yourselves, it is the gift of God -- not by works, so that no one can boast" (vv. 8-9).*

I don't think a man ever gets over football."

Especially if it's Auburn football. Walker Reynolds certainly didn't. He spoke those wistful words when he was 84, long after his playing days were over.

Reynolds played for Auburn from 1906-09, serving as captain his last season. He made All-Southern in 1908 as an end and played quarterback as a senior. He played in a different era on a field he said was "sandy and rocky, just about as hard as a paved street. There was no grass. You got skinned up on that field at the first of the year, and you stayed skinned up the whole year." The field had only temporary stands, and six thousand was a big crowd for a game. "We wouldn't have that many unless it was a pretty good game," Reynolds recalled.

He furnished his own helmet, soft leather that may have been lined with either cotton or wool. "As I remember, most of us furnished our own uniforms. I think they furnished shoes," Reynolds remembered. He had no scholarship, and so to help with expenses, Reynolds set up a store his senior year and sold athletic supplies and suits.

The team traveled on the train, and the alums rode with them.

# TIGERS

The biggest annoyance was cinders blowing into the cars.

His coach, Mike Donahue, had only one assistant and took in "country boys who had never played football and made players out of them."

This was a long time ago, an era foreign to today's players and fans when "there were one or two cars in Auburn," a big thrill was watching the train go by, and the War Eagle battle cry had not yet appeared. But Walker Reynolds never got over Auburn football.

Some things in life have a way of getting under your skin and never letting go. Your passion may have begun the first time you rode in a convertible. Or when your breath was taken away the first time you saw the one who would become your spouse. You knew you were hooked the first time you walked into Jordan-Hare Stadium on game day.

You can put God's love on that list, too. Once you encounter it in the person of Jesus Christ, you never get over it. That's because when you really and sincerely give your life to Jesus by acknowledging him as the Lord of your life, God's love – his grace – changes you. It sets you free to live in peace and in joy, free from the fear of death's apparent victory.

When you meet Jesus, you're never the same again. You just never get over the experience.

*Auburn is a tradition in my family.*
*-- Walker Reynolds, Captain 1909*

**Some things hit you so hard you're never the same again; meeting Jesus is like that.**

# SMALL SEEDS

### Read Mark 4:21-32.

*"'[The kingdom of God] is like a mustard seed, which is the smallest seed you plant in the ground. Yet when planted, it grows and becomes the largest of all garden plants'" (vv. 31-32).*

**A** trip to Memphis in 1967 started it all.

"It" is women's varsity competition at Auburn. Five years before the passage of Title IX, the women's PE department received an invitation to a volleyball tournament in Memphis, and everyone agreed it was a great idea. So Sandra Bridges (Newkirk), Auburn's intramural coordinator and a PE teacher, was given the job of putting together a team. She was to be the volleyball coach for the next 13 years.

To say it was a shoestring operation is being kind. The players who made that fateful trip to Tennessee furnished their own white shorts and blue Auburn T-shirts. As the squad got ready to play its first match, officials told Newkirk numbers were required on the jerseys. So the players and their coach assembled numbers from tape.

Newkirk remembered that the "kids paid their own way. The only thing the university covered the first several years were the tournament entry fees." She recalled that team members sold stationery and cookies for extra traveling money. Not until 1970 did the team have uniforms. When the team made the national

tournament in 1980, the squad traveled to Lawrence, Kan., in cars and stayed at the home of a player's aunt. "We had 15 people in one lady's house," Newkirk recalled. The second day the team got snowed in, couldn't get back to the house, and had to spend the night at the home of a University of Kansas professor. The players had only their uniforms and warmups.

That was the beginning, but, oh, just look at women's athletics at Auburn today.

Most worthwhile aspects of life take time and tending to grow from small beginnings into something magnificent. A good marriage is that way. Your beautiful lawn just didn't appear. Old friends get that way after years of cultivation. And children don't get to be responsible and caring adults overnight.

Your faith, too, must be nurtured over time. Remember those older folks you revered as saints when you were growing up? Such distinction is achieved, not awarded. That is, they didn't start out that way. They were mature Christians because they walked and talked with Jesus; they prayed; they studied God's word; they helped others. They nourished and tended their faith with constant, loving care and attention.

In your faith as in other areas of your life, it's OK to start small. Faith is a journey, not a destination. You keep growing as those saints did, always moving on to bigger and better things in God.

*We were happy with everything we got.*
  *-- Sandra Bridges Newkirk on the early days of Auburn volleyball*

**Faith is a lifelong journey of growth.**

DAY 58

# DRY RUN

### Read 1 Kings 16:29-17:1, 18:1.

*"Elijah the Tishbite, from Tishbe in Gilead, said to Ahab, 'As the Lord, the God of Israel, lives, whom I serve, there shall be neither dew nor rain in the next few years except at my word'" (v. 17:1).*

The drought was of biblical proportions; it lasted nine years.

On one glorious afternoon in November 1982, it ended at Legion Field. Bound for the Tangerine Bowl, the Auburn Tigers defeated Alabama 23-22. The win ended for the Auburn faithful what Don Kausler, Jr. of *The Birmingham News* described as nine years of "humility, frustration, agony and emptiness, nine years of having to plug their ears and hold their tongues while those big-mouths from across the state could gloat." The Tigers had lost to the hated Crimson Tide nine straight times.

The drought appeared headed right into a decade for the first three quarters. Alabama rolled up 23 first downs to Auburn's six and outgained the Tigers 445-132, but Auburn trailed only 22-14 as the final quarter began. "Everybody realized it was still within our reach," quarterback Randy Campbell said.

Turned out it was. A 53-yard run by a freshman named Bo Jackson set up Al Del Greco's 23-yard field goal to make it 22-17 with 9:06 left. The Tiger defense then forced an Alabama punt, and the offense drove 66 yards to win it. Jackson's legendary over-the-top score from the one came with 2:26 to play.

# TIGERS

Auburn actually had to clinch the win twice. Safety Bob Harris intercepted a pass with 1:45 left, but with 1:09 left, Auburn fumbled to give Alabama new life. "I felt, 'Oh, no. This can't happen,'" Campbell said. This was one Auburn wasn't going to lose, though. A sack and a penalty doused Alabama's last hopes for a miracle.

The drought was over.

You can walk across that river you boated on in the spring. The city's put all neighborhoods on water restriction, and that beautiful lawn you fertilized and seeded will turn a sickly, pale green and may lapse all the way to brown. Somebody wrote "Wash Me" on the rear window of your truck.

The sun bakes everything, including the concrete. The earth itself seems exhausted, just barely hanging on. It's a drought.

It's the way a soul looks that shuts God out.

God instilled thirst in us to warn us of our body's need for physical water. He also gave us a spiritual thirst that can be quenched only by his presence in our lives. Without God, we are like tumbleweeds, dried out and windblown, offering the illusion of life where there is only death.

Living water – water of life – is readily available in Jesus. We may drink our fill, and thus we slake our thirst and end our soul's drought – forever.

*Drink before you are thirsty. Rest before you are tired.*
*-- Paul de Vivie, father of French cycle touring*

**Our souls thirst for the refreshing presence of God.**

# MIRACLE PLAYS

### Read Matthew 12:38-42.

*"He answered, 'A wicked and adulterous generation asks for a miraculous sign!'" (v. 39)*

**W**hat happened in the fourth quarter will live in Auburn glory and LSU infamy." Thus was described the miraculous finish of the 1994 LSU game.

LSU had the ball and a 23-9 lead, and Auburn defensive coordinator Wayne Hall knew how much trouble the Tigers were in. He remembered thinking, "If they run the ball right then, the game is over."

But LSU threw, and safety Ken Alvis got the Tigers back in the game when he returned an interception 42 yards for a touchdown to make it 23-16 with 12:14 left.

Hall said LSU threw because "in their minds, if they make a first down, the game is over. Still, I am sitting there saying, 'Please throw the ball. Give us one more chance.'" They did, and cornerback Fred Smith proceeded to nab an interception and take it all the way. The game was tied at 23.

The Bayou Bengals appeared to have escaped when they kicked a field goal and got the ball back, but they proved themselves to be slow learners.

On third down with less than two minutes to play, they threw a pass. Linebacker Jason Miska tipped the pass, and safety Brian Robinson was the hero this time. He snared the interception and

ran 41 untouched yards for the third defensive touchdown of the quarter, thrusting one finger into the air in celebration as he crossed the goal line. In what Hall called the most remarkable game he was ever a part of, the Tigers had a miraculous 30-26 win.

Miracles defy rational explanation – like three fourth-quarter scores on interceptions to pull off a miraculous comeback. Or escaping with minor abrasions from an accident that totals your car. Or recovering from an illness that seemed terminal. Underlying the notion of miracles is that they are rare instances of direct divine intervention that reveal God.

But life shows us quite the contrary, that miracles are anything but rare. Since God made the world and everything in it, everything around you is miraculous. Even you are a miracle. Your life thus can be mundane, dull, and ordinary, or it can be spent in a glorious attitude of childlike wonder and awe.

It depends on whether or not you see the world through the eyes of faith; only through faith can you discern the hand of God in any event. Only through faith can you see the miraculous and thus see God.

Jesus knew that miracles don't produce faith, but rather faith produces miracles.

*Do you believe in miracles? Yes!*
*– Broadcaster Al Michaels when U.S. defeated USSR in hockey in 1980*
*Winter Games*

**Miracles are all around us,**
**but it takes the eyes of faith to see them.**

# FOOD FOR THOUGHT

**Read Genesis 9:1-7.**

*"Everything that lives and moves will be food for you. Just as I gave you the green plants, I now give you everything"* *(v. 3).*

The mere mention of a football team's training table conjures up images of mounds of potatoes and piles of steak being consumed ravenously by mammoth young men.

The oversized players of today do indeed dispose of staggering amounts of victuals. Even in the early days of college football, though, when players were smaller, the athletes routinely ate more than their fair share of food. One Georgia lineman in 1916 had a daily breakfast that consisted of "11 fried eggs, a quart of milk, a fried chicken, and a dozen biscuits."

During the 1897 football season, a sparse pre-game meal was blamed for a poor Auburn performance when the Tigers played two games in two days. Auburn whipped the University of Nashville 18-4 on Friday, the yearbook grumbling that Nashville's score was "made on a grossly erroneous decision of the umpire."

After the game, "the team was rushed right from the dressing-room to the train, direct for Sewanee, where they arrived Saturday morning, after having traveled over five hundred miles and played a hard game the day before – tired, hungry and sleepy." The little town didn't have a hotel, though, and a training table was unavailable, so the team was taken to private houses "for

# TIGERS

what was termed dinner." Again registering its unhappiness, the yearbook sniffed that the meal consisted of "pleasant smiles, boiled rice, toothpicks, and water. As everyone knows, football cannot be played on such a diet. The game resulted in neither side scoring." Incensed by the food and the tie, the writer told Sewanee "Auburn has held the championship over you for two consecutive years, despite your endeavors to rob us of the game."

Belly up to the buffet, boys and girls, for barbecue, sirloin steak, grilled chicken, and fried catfish with hush puppies. Rachael Ray's a household name; hamburger joints, pizza parlors, and taco stands lurk on every corner; and we have a TV channel devoted exclusively to food. We love our chow.

Food is one of God's really good ideas, but consider the complex divine plan that gets those French fries to your mouth. The creator of all life devised a system in which living things are sustained and nourished physically through the sacrifice of other living things in a way similar to what Christ underwent to save you spiritually. Whether it's fast food or home-cooked, everything you eat is a gift from God secured through a divine plan in which some plants and animals have given up their lives.

Pausing to give thanks before you dive in seems the least you can do.

*I cut down to six meals a day.*
                                    *-- Charles Barkley on losing weight*

**God created a system that nourishes you
through the sacrifice of other living things;
that's worth a thank-you.**

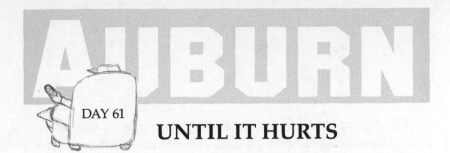

# UNTIL IT HURTS

### Read Isaiah 53.

*"He was despised and rejected by men, a man of sorrows, and familiar with suffering" (v. 3a).*

**A**drienne Binder came to Auburn because when she visited, she saw agony — and she wanted to be a part of it.

Binder is a legendary part of Auburn's legendary women's swimming program, a key member of the national championship teams of 2004, 2006, and 2007. Her resume includes 14-time All-American honors, NCAA champion in the 500 freestyle, four-time SEC champion, SEC record holder, silver medalist in the World University Games, bronze medalist in the Goodwill Games, and a spot on the 2007 U.S. Pan American games squad.

Binder even made the SEC Academic Honor Roll, and in the football-crazed state of Alabama, she was so remarkable that the U.S. Sports Academy once named her Alabama's Athlete of the Month.

But Binder is from a tight-knit California family, and her older sister swam for Southern California. She was highly recruited out of high school, so Auburn needed something special to lure her 2,000 miles away from home to the Loveliest Village. As it turned out, the Tigers had that something special: suffering to an extreme.

Binder said that what clinched Auburn for her on her recruiting trip was the sheer agony she saw the Tiger swimmers going

through in their training, reputed to be the toughest strength and conditioning workouts of any sport at Auburn. "I saw it and I was in awe," she said. "I was like, 'I want to do that.' It has a lot to do with bonding and coming together as a team. You see people falling and breaking down and their teammates are there to bring them back up. It's something unique to our program that makes Auburn pretty special."

If you say so.

Unlike the Auburn swimmers, we don't usually include actual physical pain and suffering as part of the price we are willing to pay for what we want. We do our best, in fact, to avoid agony. Okay, we'll work overtime, often when it means we neglect our family. We'll relocate when a job promotion requires it. We'll even go back to school. But actual pain, suffering, and agony? What would we give up to avoid that? Everything?

Merely by choosing to, Jesus could have easily evaded the horrific pain and suffering he underwent. Instead, he opted for his love for you over his own well-being, and agony was part of his decision for love.

Now we all face the question: How far do we go with Jesus? Do we bail out on him when it gets inconvenient? Or do we walk with him all the way even when it hurts – just as Jesus did for us?

*Sometimes you have to play with a little pain.*
*— Clemson running back C.J. Spiller*

**We must decide whether we'll walk all the way**
**with Jesus, even when it hurts, or whether**
**we'll stop when faith gets inconvenient.**

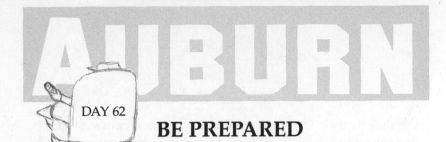

# BE PREPARED

**Read Matthew 10:5-23.**

*"I am sending you out like sheep among wolves. Therefore be as shrewd as snakes and as innocent as doves" (v. 16).*

**B**e prepared. It's what a Boy Scout would say. It's also what former coach Pat Dye said to the Auburn coaching staff the week of the Alabama game of 2000.

At the 9 a.m. staff meeting on Monday before the game, "a man in a weathered baseball hat, muddy work boots, and Wranglers amble[d] into the meeting room." It was Dye, who regularly visited the coaching staff during the season. He could deliver some perspective to Coach Tommy Tuberville and his assistant coaches, who were making their first visit to Tuscaloosa.

The coach who emphasized that his team would never be outworked or unprepared indeed had something to say. The key, he said, was to let Alabama know Auburn was not afraid to play in Tuscaloosa. He conceded Alabama had more talent; he conceded Auburn would struggle not to be intimidated as the team drove down Bryant Avenue. "They were picked to win this conference. They got all the talent and ability," Dye said.

So how could the Tigers overcome Alabama's advantages? "Preparation is key," Dye said. "Be prepared, mentally and physically." The preparation, he said, would enable the Tigers to take advantage of Alabama's weaknesses when the pressure was on late in the game. "If you're winning, plan how you're going to

handle it. If you're losing, it's not the end of the world either," Dye said.

Coach Tuberville and his staff certainly had their team prepared for that 2000 game. Auburn shut out the Tide for the first time since 1987 and won 9-0.

You know the importance of preparation in your own life. You went to the bank for a car loan, facts and figures in hand. That presentation you made at work was seamless because you practiced. The kids' school play suffered no meltdowns because they rehearsed. Knowing what you need to do and doing what you must to succeed isn't luck; it's preparation.

Jesus understood this, and he prepared his followers by lecturing them and by sending them on field trips. Two thousand years later, the life of faith requires similar training and study. You prepare so you'll be ready when that unsaved neighbor standing beside you at your backyard grill asks about Jesus. You prepare so you will know how God wants you to live. You prepare so you are certain in what you believe when the secular, godless world challenges it.

And one day you'll see God face to face. You certainly want to be prepared for that.

*Spectacular achievements are always preceded by unspectacular preparation.*

*-- Roger Staubach*

**Living in faith requires constant study
and training, preparation for the day
when you meet God face to face.**

# AUTHORITY FIGURE

### Read Psalm 95:1-7a.

*"Come, let us bow down in worship, let us kneel before the Lord" (v. 6).*

**H**eisman Trophy-winner Pat Sullivan challenged Coach Shug Jordan's authority once. But only once.

The first season of the legendary Sullivan-to-Terry-Beasley combination was 1969. The super sophs led the Tigers to an 8-2 record, including a 49-26 whacking of Alabama, the most points scored on Alabama since 1907.

Sullivan's brief life as a rebel occurred in the Bluebonnet Bowl that followed the season. The Tigers were trailing the Houston Cougars and faced fourth and one on their own 35. Jordan decided to punt, but when he sent the kicker into the game, Sullivan sent him back out and called a play. The gamble failed when the Tigers didn't make the first down.

Sullivan probably didn't want to face his coach right about then, and he recalled that "Coach Jordan met me as I came off the field, and in a very calm manner he put his arm around my shoulder." Quite patiently and calmly, Jordan pointed out that his star quarterback must not have understood; he wanted a punt. "Yes, sir, but I felt we should go for it," Sullivan replied.

Jordan's entire demeanor changed. "His comforting arm around my shoulder became more of a vise grip around my neck," Sullivan remembered. "Then he told me in no uncertain terms to

# TIGERS

go sit on the bench and not get up until the game was over."

Even the team's star, who would eventually be named the best college player in America, could not challenge Coach Jordan's authority and get away with it. On Shug Jordan's Auburn teams, there was only one boss and he was it; everyone else did what the boss said.

Stand up for yourself. Be your own person. Cherish your independence. That's what the world tells us. Naively, we may believe it and plan to live just that way – until we grow up and discover that authority figures don't take kindly to being challenged by those under their supervision or direction.

Our basic survival skills kick in, and we change our tune: play along, don't rock the boat, be a company person. We become – gasp! – obedient, dampening our rebelliousness on behalf of what we perceive to be a greater purpose.

Our relationship with God is similar in that he demands obedience from us. We believe in and trust what Jesus told us as the revealed word of God, and then we are obedient to it.

Obedience – even to God -- is not easy for us. It vexes us -- at least until we learn that what we surrender in independence to God is meaningless compared to the blessings we receive from him in return.

*Football is like life; it requires perseverance, self-denial, hard work, sacrifice, dedication, and respect for authority.*

*– Vince Lombardi*

**God seeks our obedience out of a loving desire to provide us with rich, purposeful, and joyous lives.**

DAY 64

# KNOW-IT-ALLS

**Read Matthew 13:10-17.**

*"The knowledge of the secrets of the kingdom of heaven has been given to you" (v. 11).*

One of Auburn's greatest football victories ever came about not because of superior talent or a great game plan but primarily because of a secret weapon: knowledge.

Many Tiger fans familiar with Auburn's football history may rightfully claim that a win in 1942 ranks right up there as one for the ages. The Tigers of 1942 managed only a 6-4-1 record, losing along the way to Ga. Tech, Florida, and Miss. State. Included among those six victories, however, was a stunning 27-13 win over the Georgia Bulldogs, who went to the Rose Bowl.

Georgia came into the game ranked number one in the nation. The Tigers had lost to Florida 6-0, while Georgia had massacred the Gators 72-0. But those four Auburn losses and the tie had a common factor that was missing in the Georgia game: They were all played in the mud and the muck. With players such as guard Vic Costellos at 167 pounds and tackle Jim McClurkin at 181 pounds, the Tigers were described as "simply too light to cope with big teams on wet fields."

Auburn also had an advantage Georgia didn't know about. An assistant coach named Shug Jordan had scouted the Bulldogs, and had "discovered a slight mannerism that was a tip-off as to whether [Georgia's great Frank] Sinkwich was going to pass

or run." Armed with that knowledge, the Auburn defense held Sinkwich to 31 yards on 21 rushes, including a fumble in his own end zone that was recovered by Fagan Canzoneri for the upset-clinching Auburn touchdown.

For the Tigers, knowledge was power – and a stunning win.

We can never know too much. We once thought our formal education ended when we entered the workplace, but now we have constant training sessions, conferences, and seminars to keep us current whether our expertise is in auto mechanics or medicine. Many areas require graduate degrees now as we scramble to stay abreast of new discoveries and information. And still we never know it all.

Nowhere, however, is the paucity of our knowledge more stark than it is when we consider God. We will never know even a fraction of all there is to apprehend about the creator of the universe – with one important exception. God has revealed all we need to know about the kingdom of Heaven to ensure our salvation. He has opened to us great and eternal secrets.

All we need to know about getting into Heaven is right there in the Bible. With God, ignorance is no excuse and knowledge that yields faith is salvation.

*I've never known a day when I didn't learn something new about this game.*

*– Connie Mack on baseball*

**When it comes to our salvation, we can indeed know it all because God has revealed to us everything we need to know.**

# THE BEAUTIFUL PEOPLE

**Read Matthew 23:23-28.**

*"Woe to you, teachers of the law and Pharisees, you hypocrites! You are like whitewashed tombs, which look beautiful on the outside, but on the inside are full of dead men's bones and everything unclean" (v. 27).*

**N**ah, she's a glamour girl." That was Charlton Young's response when his dad asked him about dating a young woman named Carolyn Jones.

Jones is indeed one of the world's beautiful people; she is also one of the greatest basketball players in Auburn's history. She was All-America in 1990 and 1991, the first two-time Player of the Year in SEC history, and a member of the 1992 U.S. Olympic team that won a bronze medal. Her jersey number, 21, was retired in 2001.

She is Auburn's career leader in free throws attempted and made, in career free-throw percentage, and in three-point field goal percentage. She averaged 18.3 points per game, second in school history. Though she played only three seasons, she is fourth all-time with 1,831 points.

About that "glamour girl" bit. Young was an administrative assistant at Auburn when he noticed Jones on TV, but he was two steps behind his dad, who had also spotted her and followed up by going to a game early and meeting her. He then asked his son if he had "ever thought about that girl Carolyn Jones." Young responded, "Nah, she's a glamour girl." But Young's dad kept

nagging his son about her until Young relented, saying, "Let me see what happens."

Some time passed while Jones played basketball in Italy before they met for the first time. They got off to a rocky start with Jones declaring, "I couldn't stand him." Young, though, was smitten by the glamour girl and persisted. They married in 1998.

Remember the brunette who sat behind you in history class? Or the blonde in English? And how about that hunk from the next apartment who washes his car every Saturday morning and just forces you to get outside earlier than you really want to?

We do love those beautiful people.

It is worth remembering amid our adulation of superficial beauty that *Vogue* or *People* probably wouldn't have been too enamored of Jesus' looks. Isaiah 53 declares that our savior "had no beauty or majesty to attract us to him, nothing in his appearance that we should desire him."

Though Jesus never urged folks to walk around with body odor and unwashed hair, he did admonish us to avoid being overly concerned with physical beauty, which fades with age despite tucks and Botox. What matters to God is inner beauty, which reveals itself in the practice of justice, mercy, and faith, and which is not only lifelong but eternal.

*Ah, the glories of women's sports: the camaraderie. The quiet dignity. The proud refusal to buy into traditional stereotypes of beauty.*
-- Sports Illustrated for Women

**When it comes to looking good to God,
it's what's inside that counts.**

# MIDDLE OF NOWHERE

### Read Genesis 28:10-22.

*"When Jacob awoke from his sleep, he thought, 'Surely the Lord is in this place, and I was not aware of it'" (v. 16).*

If you've never been to Auburn, can you find it? Eric Shore couldn't.

On Oct. 5, 2005, Shore became the winningest men's tennis coach in Auburn history with his 193rd win. The wins have kept piling up since then, making Auburn one of the country's top programs. Under Shore's leadership through the 2010 season, the Tigers had qualified for eleven straight NCAA tournaments and sixteen of the last eighteen.

All those wins and all that success were ahead of Shore in 1990 when he went looking for Auburn and couldn't find it. A native of Ottawa, Shore was trying to find Auburn to apply for the head coaching job. As he drove down I-85, he was looking for a sign that would point him toward Auburn. And he kept looking.

Shore said, "I'd flown into Atlanta, and there were no signs for Auburn. None. I was like 'Where the heck is this place?' I had to pull over at a gas station and ask where Auburn was. I thought I'd missed it."

An assistant at South Carolina for five years, Shore confessed he "had no idea where Auburn was." All he knew was that a Southeastern Conference school needed a head tennis coach. "I'd heard about it, but I didn't know if it was in Alabama or Georgia."

# TIGERS

When he finally found the Loveliest Village, Shore knew he was home. "My first impression was how unbelievably pretty it was," he said. "That first time here, something struck me as unique about the place. Auburn is different. You can't describe it. You just have to come and experience it." Even if you can't get to it without stopping for directions at a gas station.

Ever been to Sulligent? Or Wadley? How about Campbell, just up the road from Salitpa? And don't miss Millerville if you're on the way to Goodwater.

They are among the many small communities, some of them nothing more than crossroads, that dot the Alabama countryside. Off the interstates and often more than a few miles from a good-sized town, they seem to be in the middle of nowhere, the type of place Eric Shore or anyone else might really need a road map to find. They're just hamlets we zip through on our way to somewhere important.

But don't be misled: Those villages are indeed special and wonderful. That's because God is in Brantley and Holly Pond just as he is in Auburn. Even when you are far off the roads well traveled, you are with God. As Jacob discovered one rather astounding morning, the middle of nowhere is, in fact, holy ground -- because God is there.

*The middle of nowhere is the place that teaches you that crossing the goal line first is not as important as the course you took to get there.*
*– Dive instructor Ridlon Kiphart*

**No matter how far off the beaten path you travel, you are still on holy ground because God is there.**

# TEN TO REMEMBER

**Read Exodus 20:1-17.**

*"God spoke all these words: 'I am the Lord your God . . . .
You shall have no other gods before me'" (vv. 1, 3).*

Try this score on for size: 94-0.

That's the score of the greatest slaughter in Auburn's long and storied football history. It came in 1894 against Georgia Tech and was Auburn's sixth football win in its third season of play. This was the first season of a new rule requiring kickoffs to travel ten yards to be legal.

A newspaper recounted the way the teams looked before the game in an age when helmetless players let their hair grow long for protection: "The Tiger-nosed Auburnites, with their ferocious and astounding shocks of hair, looked anxious and ready for the fray, while the Tech boys appeared nervous." The players from Atlanta apparently realized what was in store for them.

Auburn has had quite a few laughers since the first game in 1892, but nothing to top that Tech score. Rounding out the ten greatest margins of victory for Auburn are these games: a 92-0 whipping of Mercer in 1916 in which Coach Mike Donahue's younger brother, Bill, carried the ball only five times but scored four touchdowns (The team also featured end Upshaw "Sad Custard" Gibson, perhaps the most colorful nickname in Auburn history.); 1920's 88-0 defeat of Howard in which Ed Shirling scored five touchdowns; the 78-0 stomping of Howard in 1910 during

a season in which the Auburn defense pitched six shutouts in seven games; 77-0 wins over Erskine in 1932 and Washington & Lee in 1920, the latter a game the Auburn players thought they would lose because W&L had an All-America and no one on the team had ever played against one; another lambasting of Howard, 72-0 in 1922; a 1917 68-0 waxing of Florida; and a pair of 63-0 wins, over Georgia Tech in 1899 and Mercer in 1907.

For Auburn fans, this is a list of ten scores to remember.

You've got your list and you're ready to go: a gallon of paint and a water hose from the hardware store; chips, peanuts, and sodas from the grocery store for tonight's card game with your buddies; the tickets for the band concert. Your list helps you remember.

God made a list once of things he wanted you to remember: the Ten Commandments. Just as your list reminds you to do something, so does God's list remind you of how you are to act in your dealings with other people and with him.

A life dedicated to Jesus is a life devoted to relationships, and God's list emphasizes that the social life and the spiritual life of the faithful cannot be sundered. God's relationship to you is one of unceasing, unqualified love, and you are to mirror that divine love in your relationships with others.

In case you forget, you have a list.

*Society today treats the Ten Commandments as if they were the ten suggestions. Never compromise on right or wrong.*
*-- College baseball coach Gordie Gillespie*

**God's list is a set of instructions on how you are to conduct yourself with other people and with him.**

# ANIMAL MAGNETISM

### Read Psalm 139:1-18.

*"For you created my inmost being; you knit me together in my mother's womb. I praise you because I am fearfully and wonderfully made" (vv. 13-14).*

At the Battle of the Wilderness in Virginia in 1864, a wounded Auburn student was left on the battlefield for dead. Thus arose one of the greatest of Auburn legends.

The student, fighting for Gen. Robert E. Lee, regained consciousness to see only two living things: himself and a baby eagle. The young soldier took the wounded bird with him, nursed it back to health, and eventually regained his own health. When the war ended, the student returned to Auburn. With him he brought the bird, now called War Eagle because of the circumstances under which he had been found.

The student ultimately became a faculty member, and he was present at Piedmont Park in Atlanta in 1892 when Auburn played its first football game ever, against Georgia. As usual, War Eagle was with him.

According to "The Fable of War Eagle," "When Auburn scored the first touchdown the old eagle broke free from its master and began to soar above the field. Auburn people looked skyward, saw the familiar figure, and shouted 'War Eagle.'" Thus, says the legend, one of college football's greatest battle cries was born. The story goes that after Auburn won the game 10-0, the old eagle

collapsed and died, having given all he had for the sake of an Auburn win.

The tradition continues with Nova, War Eagle VII, who flew for the first time in Auburn's 42-10 win over Kentucky in 2004. Nova officially took over as the proud symbol of the school and its athletic teams in 2006.

College sports' greatest battle cry has caused some confusion over the years from the propensity many have for referring to the Auburn War Eagles. Auburn has only one nickname: the Tigers.

Animals such as War Eagle elicit our awe and our respect. Nothing enlivens a trip more than glimpsing turkeys, bears, or deer in the wild. Admit it: You go along with the kids' trip to the zoo because you think it's a cool place too. All that variety of life is mind-boggling. Who could conceive of a golden eagle, a walrus, a moose, or a prairie dog? Who could possibly have that rich an imagination?

But the next time you're in a crowd, look around at the parade of faces. Who could come up with the idea for all those different people? For that matter, who could conceive of you? You are unique, a masterpiece who will never be duplicated.

The master creator, God Almighty, is behind it all. He thought of you and brought you into being. If you had a manufacturer's label, it might say, "Lovingly handmade in Heaven by #1 -- God."

*There's a closeness that all Auburn people feel. It's the war eagle spirit.*
*-- Shug Jordan*

**You may consider some painting a work of art,**
**but the real masterpiece is you.**

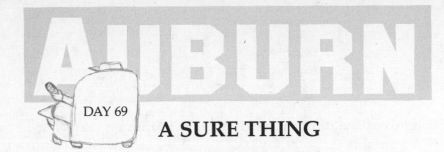

# A SURE THING

**Read Romans 8:28-30.**

*"We know that in all things God works for the good of those who love him, who have been called according to his purpose" (v. 28).*

They went through two losing seasons, two coaching changes, and three head coaches. The only certainty in their football life at Auburn was uncertainty.

They were the fourteen Auburn football seniors of the class of 2001. Coach Tommy Tuberville spoke of what they had endured and had lost after they came off the practice field for the last time in preparation for the 2001 Citrus Bowl game against Michigan. He called them "the perfect example of perseverance and sacrifice. They really went through some uncertain times," the head coach said. "When you're a junior or senior and you have a change in coaching staff, those two classes really get cheated."

Tuberville so appreciated what the seniors had gone through and had meant to the new coaching staff that he took the time at the last practice to thank them. "They've worked hard to make this thing a lot better for Auburn University," he said.

Senior quarterback Ben Leard agreed it hadn't been easy for them. "We have overcome a lot," he said. "As the season comes to a close, we'll sit around and reminisce about the good times and the bad times." Despite all the turmoil and the uncertainty they endured, all the testing of their character and their ability

# TIGERS

to persevere, Leard probably spoke for the whole group when he said, "We wish we had one more season to play with each other and to play as an Auburn Tiger."

But they didn't.

Football games aren't played on paper. That is, you attend an Auburn game expecting the Tigers to win, but you don't know for sure. If you did, why bother to go? Any football game worth watching carries with it an element of uncertainty.

Life doesn't get played on paper either, which means that living, too, comes laden with uncertainty. You never know what's going to happen tomorrow or even an hour from now. Oh, sure, you think you know. For instance, right now you may be certain that you'll be at work Monday morning or that you'll have a job next month. Life's uncertainties, though, can intervene at any time and disrupt your nice, pat expectations.

Ironically, while you can't know for sure about this afternoon, you can know for certain about forever. Eternity is a sure thing because it's in God's hands. Your unwavering faith and God's sure promises lock in a certain future for you.

And those fourteen players who endured all that turmoil and uncertainty? Along the way, they won two SEC Western Division titles.

*There is nothing in life so uncertain as a sure thing.*
*-- NHL Coach Scotty Bowman*

**Life is unpredictable, and tomorrow is uncertain;**
**only eternity is a sure thing**
**because God controls it.**

# GOOD SPORTS

**Read Titus 2:1-8.**

*"Show integrity, seriousness and soundness of speech that
cannot be condemned, so that those who oppose you may
be ashamed because they have nothing bad to say about
us" (vv. 7b, 8).*

**A**uburn's 1922 football team demonstrated one of the greatest
and most unique acts of sportsmanship in any game in any era.

The squad was one of Mike Donahue's better teams; it was, in
fact, his last Auburn team as he resigned at season's end. They
went 8-2 in this age before the SEC, defeating the likes of Marion,
Howard, Spring Hill, Mercer, the Praying Colonels of Centre
College, and Fort Benning. They did whip Georgia 7-3 and Tulane
19-0.

They lost to Army 19-6 in a game in which Auburn captain
John Shirey, incensed at what he felt was unnecessary roughness
by the Cadets, offered "to fight single-handedly not only the
military academy, but the combined forces of the United States."
The second loss came to Georgia Tech 14-6 in the last game of
the season before the largest crowd in the history of Southern
intercollegiate football. At that game, the team did something
extraordinary.

Tech's star was Red Barron, who scored a touchdown in that
win over the Tigers. Barron was married that afternoon, and the
Auburn team presented Barron with a silver service as a wedding

present!

Slick Moulton, one of Auburn's all-time great ends, said, "We liked to have never paid for that silver service. We nickled up and dimed up."

The team displayed more sportsmanship during the game. Barron played with a broken jaw, and Moulton said, "Coach Donahue told us not to ever tackle him high, to tackle him low. He had legs like a mule, but we never hit his face."

One of life's paradoxes is that many who would never consider cheating on the tennis court or the racquetball court to gain an advantage think nothing of doing so in other areas of their life. In other words, the good sportsmanship they practice on the golf course or on the Monopoly board doesn't carry over. They play with the truth, cut corners, abuse others verbally, run roughshod over the weaker, and generally cheat whenever they can to gain an advantage on the job or in their personal relationships.

But good sportsmanship is a way of living, not just of playing. Shouldn't you accept defeat without complaint (You don't have to like it.); win gracefully without gloating; treat your competition with fairness, courtesy, generosity, and respect? That's the way one team treats another in the name of sportsmanship. That's the way one person treats another in the name of Jesus.

*One person practicing sportsmanship is better than a hundred teaching it.*

-- *Knute Rockne*

**Sportsmanship -- treating others with courtesy, fairness, and respect -- is a way of living, not just a way of playing.**

# A JOYFUL NOISE

**Read Psalm 100.**

*"Make a joyful noise to the Lord, all the earth" (v. 1 NRSV).*

If it's game day at Jordan-Hare it must be noisy, and the most raucous and loudest noisemakers of them all will be a group that began with a dozen or so guys and one horn named Jenny Lind: the Auburn University Marching Band.

The Auburn band had its origins in the twelve-cadet drum corps of the 19th century. In 1897, M. Thomas Fullan, a mechanical arts instructor, realized that an instrumental college band would be an improvement. While the first band members waited for instruments to arrive, they relied on "an old brass tenor horn dubbed 'Jenny Lind.' . . . The ten or twelve boys lined up in 'barber shop' manner, waiting for their turn with 'Jenny Lind.'"

The Auburn band actually participated in World War I under the name of the 16th Infantry Regimental Band. In 1917, Director P.R. "Bedie" Bidez -- known to his band members as "Chief" -- led the band across the Rhine River into Germany to the tune of "Glory to Ole Auburn" to celebrate the Allied victory.

Bidez, by the way, had his moment of glory on the gridiron. Short on fullbacks, Coach Mike Donahue telegraphed Bidez, a member of the scrub team (today's scout team), to join the team in Birmingham for the 1913 Vanderbilt game. Bidez ran three times and scored in the 14-6 Auburn win.

# TIGERS

One of the band's biggest changes occurred in 1946 with the addition of female majorettes. Coeds began playing instruments in 1950.

In 2004, the Auburn band won the Sudler Intercollegiate Marching Band Trophy, the equivalent of the Heisman Trophy for college bands, which firmly established its national reputation for excellence.

On game day, nobody quite makes a joyful noise the way the Auburn University Marching Band does.

Maybe you can't play a lick or carry a tune in the proverbial bucket. Or perhaps you do know your way around a guitar or a keyboard and can sing "Sweet Home Alabama" on karaoke night without closing the joint down.

Unless you're a professional musician, however, how well you play or sing really doesn't matter. What counts is that you have music in your heart and sometimes you have to turn it loose – especially when the Tigers score and the Auburn band plays.

That same boisterous and noisy enthusiasm should also be a part of the joy you have in your worship of God. Making "a joyful noise" to the Lord means just that, bursting forth in a racket for God. When you consider that God loves you and always will, how can you help but shout, holler, and sing – or even whisper -- your love in return?

*I like it because it plays old music.*
*-- Pitcher Tug McGraw on his '54 Buick*

**You call it music; others may call it noise.**
**If it's joyful, send some God's way.**

# AGE BEFORE BEAUTY

**Read Psalm 92.**

*"[The righteous] will still bear fruit in old age, they will
stay fresh and green, proclaiming, 'The Lord is upright'"
(vv. 14-15).*

**H**e was 25 – and he was too old.

At least, that's what the mavens of competitive swimming said
about Rowdy Gaines, one of Auburn's truly legendary athletes,
as the 1984 Olympics neared. Gaines had done it all on The
Plains. Before he graduated in 1981, he was an eight-time NCAA
champion, including five individual championships, and held
eleven world records.

Gaines cherished his time at Auburn when his teammates
became like family. "Those memories mean more to me than
breaking records and winning gold medals," he said.

But while he was at Auburn, Gaines had his sights set on the
1980 Olympics. "The pinnacle of success for swimming is the
Olympics," he said. "That's our Super Bowl, and it only happens
once every four years." Gaines was among the American athletes
everyone predicted would bring home a whole bunch of medals.

He never got the chance. The Soviets invaded Afghanistan, and
in protest the United States withdrew from the 1980 Games in
Moscow. When the 1984 Olympics in Los Angeles rolled around,
Gaines was 25, and that's when conventional wisdom declared he
was too old by competitive swimming standards. He would never

# TIGERS

get his "Super Bowl" appearance, let alone accomplish anything.

All the "old man" of the sport did in 1984 was solidify his legacy as one of the top Olympic performers of all time by winning three gold medals. "It was a long, long journey," Gaines said. "The feeling I had was that the journey was really worth it."

He was later inducted into the U.S. Olympic Hall of Fame. Oh, yeah: "Too old" in 1984, Gaines also qualified for the Olympic trials in Atlanta – in 1996.

To consider someone old by age twenty-five is rather extreme even for our youth-obsessed culture, but we don't like to admit – even to ourselves – that we're not as young as we used to be.

So we keep plastic surgeons in business, dye our hair, buy cases of those miracle wrinkle-reducing creams, and redouble our efforts in the gym. Sometimes, though, we just have to face up to the truth the mirror tells us: We're getting older every day.

It's really all right, though, because aging and old age are part of the natural cycle of our lives, which was God's idea in the first place. God's conception of the golden years, though, doesn't include unlimited close encounters with a rocking chair and nothing more. God expects us to serve him as we are able all the days of our life. Those who serve God flourish no matter their age because the energizing power of God is in them.

*Age is a question of mind over matter. If you don't mind, it doesn't matter.*

*-- Pitcher and Philosopher Satchel Paige*

**Servants of God don't ever retire; they keep working until they get the ultimate promotion.**

# BURYING THE HATCHET

**Read 2 Corinthians 5:16-21.**

*"All this is from God, who reconciled us to himself through Christ and gave us the ministry of reconciliation" (v. 18).*

They buried the hatchet -- quite literally.

On the morning of the final Auburn football game of 1948, an unusual and important ceremony took place. The presidents of the student bodies of Alabama and Auburn met, "dug a hole in the ground in Birmingham's Woodrow Wilson Park, tossed a hatchet in, and buried it."

This literal burying of the hatchet symbolized the figurative burying that was to take place later that day when Auburn and Alabama would meet each other in football. It seems hard to believe today, but Alabama and Auburn had not played each other in football since 1907.

They had played each other for eight straight seasons, and a game was scheduled for 1908 before a dispute arose over how many players Auburn could suit up, how much expense money Auburn was to receive, and whether a Southern or an Eastern umpire should be brought in. By the time the disputes were resolved, October had arrived and the schedules were made. The series simply lapsed.

Walker Reynolds, an All-Southern end for Auburn in 1908, once called the failure to resume the series for so long "absolutely

ridiculous. It was nothing in the world but bull-headedness on the part of each side. I figure it cost Auburn a million dollars."

Former Auburn Coach Mike Donahue was among those at both schools who tried several times over the years to repair the strained relations and resume the series, but not until the burying of the hatchet in 1948 was all forgiven and forgotten.

Remember that buddy you used to go fishing with? That friend you used to roam the mall with? The one who introduced you to sushi? Remember that person who was so special you thought this might be "the one"? And now you don't even speak because of something -- who remembers exactly? -- one of you did.

Fractured relationships are as much a part of life as sunshine and aching feet. In discussing the matter of people we greet coldly if at all, Jesus' instructions were simple: forgive the other person. Admittedly, this is easier said than done for everybody except Jesus, but reconciling with others sets you free to get on with your life. Harboring a grudge is a way to self-destruction; kissing and making up is a way to inner peace and contentment.

Forgiveness, thus, is another of God's gifts to help us toward rich, full lives. Besides, you can never outforgive God, who forgives you.

*Life is short, so don't waste any of it carrying around a load of bitterness. It only sours your life, and the world won't pay any attention anyway.*

-- *Pat Dye*

**Making up with others frees you from your past, turning you loose to get on with your richer, fuller future.**

# CHEAP TRICKS

**Read Acts 19:11-20.**

*"The evil spirit answered them, 'Jesus I know, and I know about Paul, but who are you?'" (v. 15)*

**A** trick play helped the Tigers to a last-second win over FSU in 1990. Only thing was – it was the Seminoles' trick play, not Auburn's.

With two seconds left on Oct. 21, Jim Von Wyl kicked a 38-yard field goal for the 20-17 win. The game winner was set up when quarterback Stan White on fourth and eight found Herbert Casey loose in the Seminole secondary and hit him with a 21-yard strike to the FSU 18. White then ran one play to the center of the field to set up the kick and turned the game over to Von Wyl.

Auburn trailed most of the game, which apparently had belonged to FSU until Coach Bobby Bowden tried one of his legendary trick plays. The Seminoles led 17-10 in the fourth quarter and were moving for what would pretty much be the game-clinching score. Then at the Auburn 41, Bowden called for the "fumblerooskie."

Jimmy Bryan of *The Birmingham News* explained that the "fumblerooskie" is "a play in which the quarterback puts the ball down behind the center's legs and then carries out a fake. . . . An offensive guard is supposed to pick the ball up." But Auburn nose guard Walter Tate was not fooled. He recovered the "fumble," and Auburn promptly drove 57 yards to tie the game with Tony

Richardson's 19-yard run setting up Stacy Danley's score from the two with only 3:47 left.

When Auburn linebacker Ricky Sutton sacked the FSU quarterback on fourth down, the Tigers got the chance that led to the winning kick. Had FSU not tried the trick play, the Tigers may well have never gotten that chance.

The trick was on FSU; Auburn got the treat.

Scam artists are everywhere — and they love trick plays. An e-mail encourages you to send money to some foreign country to get rich. That guy at your front door offers to resurface your driveway at a ridiculously low price. A TV ad promises a pill to help you lose weight without diet or exercise.

You've been around; you check things out before deciding. The same approach is necessary with spiritual matters, too, because false religions and bogus Christian denominations abound. The key is what any group does with Jesus. Is he the son of God, the ruler of the universe, and the only way to salvation? If not, then what the group espouses is something other than the true Word of God.

The good news about Jesus does indeed sound too good to be true. But the only catch is that there is no catch. No trick -- just the truth.

*When you run trick plays and they work, you're a genius. But when they don't work, folks question your sanity.*
                                                      *-- Bobby Bowden*

**God's promises through Jesus sound too good to be true, but the only catch is that there is no catch.**

# IN THE KNOW

Read John 4:19-26, 39-42.

*"They said to the woman, . . . 'Now we have heard for ourselves, and we know that this man really is the Savior of the world'" (v. 42).*

**E**ight seconds left to play. Florida led 33-29. Auburn lined up at the Gator eight. And the game was over!

At least it was in the eyes of the only two people who mattered: Auburn quarterback Patrick Nix and receiver Frank Sanders. When they saw the Florida defense, they knew. "I'll never forget looking at Frank and Frank looking at me," Nix remembered. "It was like 'I can't believe this. This game is over. We're going to win.'"

On Oct. 15, 1994, in Gainesville, Auburn and Florida were both undefeated. Auburn had won seventeen straight, but Florida was ranked number one. Coach Steve Spurrier had never lost an SEC game in The Swamp.

And these two heavyweights put on one of the greatest shootouts in SEC history. Nix threw an incredible 51 passes, hitting 28 for 319 yards and three touchdowns. Stephen Davis rushed for 113 yards on 20 carries.

Nix had hit tight end Andy Fuller -- who had a career day with seven catches for 115 yards and a touchdown -- with a 30-yard touchdown pass in the fourth quarter to put the Tigers up 29-26, but the Gators had answered. With only 1:20 left to play, Brian

Robinson intercepted a Gator pass to give Auburn one more chance. Nix hit Thomas Bailey for fourteen yards and Willie Gosha for twenty to the eight. So it came down to that last play.

And Nix and Sanders just knew.

They just knew in the same way you know certain things in your life. That your spouse loves you, for instance. That you are good at your job. That tea should be iced and sweetened. That a bad day fishing is still better than a good day at work. That the best barbecue comes from a pig. You know these things even though no mathematician or philosopher can prove any of this on paper.

It's the same way with faith in Jesus: You just know that he is God's son and the savior of the world. You know it in the same way that you know Auburn is the only team worth pulling for: with every fiber of your being, with all your heart, your mind, and your soul.

You just know, and because you know him, Jesus knows you. And that is all you really need to know.

That touchdown pass Nix threw to Sanders to win the game? He never saw the catch. Surrounded by blitzing Gators, Nix saw Sanders go up and then lost sight of him. But he still knew: "I knew it was over. It was Frank. He was going to catch the ball." Nix didn't have to see to believe. Auburn won 36-33.

*It's what you learn after you think you know it all that counts.*
*-- Earl Weaver*

**A life of faith is lived in certainty and conviction:**
**You just know you know.**

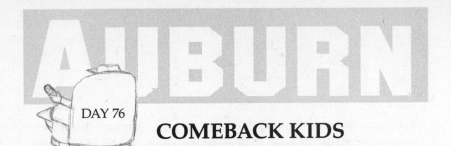

# COMEBACK KIDS

**Read Acts 9:1-22.**

*"All those who heard him were astonished and asked,*
*'Isn't he the man who raised havoc in Jerusalem among*
*those who call on this name?'" (v. 21)*

The Tigers of 2001 pulled off the greatest comeback in SEC baseball history, one called both improbable and impossible.

That season Auburn started SEC play 0-9. So what can a coach -- especially a first-year coach trying to prove himself -- say when it looks as though the season is down the tubes after only three series? Steve Renfroe gained support from the same strong faith that had carried him through tougher times in his life. "Who am I to believe I'm above any circumstances?" he once said. "I look around and I can only see blessings in my life."

So he told his team they could still make the SEC tournament field. "It could happen," he said. "I told them, 'Hey, write one for the ages.'" They would have to; no team in SEC baseball history had ever made the tournament after such a dreadful start.

But gradually the Tigers scrapped and clawed their way back into tournament contention. Still, they had to travel to mighty LSU in mid-May and take two of three the last weekend of the season to make the tournament field. So Auburn opened up like gangbusters, right? Not hardly. LSU totally humbled the Tigers 20-5 in the series opener, and then jumped out to a 5-1 lead in the second game heading into the eighth inning. The comeback

apparently wouldn't happen.

But the Tigers from Auburn rallied to score six runs in the eighth to whip the Tigers from Baton Rouge 7-5. That kept their hopes alive, but again LSU seemed to have everything under control with a lead heading into the ninth inning of the final game. Incredibly, Auburn scored five runs and won 9-7. The comeback kids were in the SEC tournament. They wrote "one for the ages."

Life will have its setbacks whether they result from personal failures or from forces and people beyond your control. Being a Christian and a faithful follower of Jesus Christ doesn't insulate you from getting into deep trouble. Maybe financial problems suffocated you. A serious illness put you on the sidelines. Or your family was hit with a great tragedy.

Life is a series of victories and defeats. Winning isn't about avoiding defeat; it's about getting back up to compete again. It's about making a comeback of your own.

When you avail yourself of God's grace and God's power, your comeback is always greater than your setback. You are never too far behind, and it's never too late in life's game for Jesus to lead you to victory, to turn trouble into triumph. As it was with the baseball Tigers of 2001 and with Paul, it's not how you start that counts; it's how you finish.

*People think only the championships are special, but it doesn't get much more special than this.*
*-- Steve Renfroe on his team's comeback in 2001*

**In life, victory is truly a matter of how you finish and whether you finish with Jesus at your side.**

# A WAY OF LIFE

## Read Romans 13:8-14.

*"The night is nearly over; the day is almost here. So let us put aside the deeds of darkness and put on the armor of light" (v. 12).*

They told him: You have to see it to believe it; Tony Levine did -- and he did.

Levine joined the Auburn football staff in March 2000 as a graduate assistant. The whole season turned out to be an eye-opening experience for him. He knew big-time college football; after all, he played wide receiver for Minnesota in the mid-90s. But nothing in his collegiate experience prepared him for his first fall in Auburn.

"This whole year has been unlike anything I've ever seen," he admitted the week of the Alabama game. "Football in Minnesota isn't anything like football in Alabama. . . . I thought this past week in playing Georgia was the most unbelievable thing I had ever seen. People stopped me in the hall this weekend and said, 'You think that was big, wait until Saturday.'" Saturday – and Levine's first-ever Iron Bowl. "In Minnesota, we thought Minnesota-Wisconsin was a big deal. It doesn't compare to this."

When Levine's family came down during the season, he tried to prepare them. He warned them, "You can't see grass on our campus for a home game" because of the parked cars. Still, "they couldn't picture it. I told my dad that there have been campers

here since Tuesday. They can't imagine it." Just think how bewildered his mom must have been when Levine spoke of closing streets off so people could throw toilet paper over trees. "They really couldn't picture that."

And the toilet paper flew after the 2000 Iron Bowl as Auburn whipped Alabama 9-0.

Tony Levine and his family learned that at Auburn, football isn't a hobby or a game; it's a way of life.

You have a way of life that defines and describes you. You're a die-hard Auburn fan for starters. Maybe you're married with a family. A city guy or a small-town gal. You wear jeans or a suit to work every day. And then there's your faith.

For the Christian, following Jesus more than anything else defines for the world your way of life. It's basically simple in its concept even if it is downright daunting in its execution. You act toward others in a way that would not embarrass you were your day to be broadcast on Fox News. You think about others in a way that would not humiliate you should your thoughts be the plotline for a new CBS sitcom.

You make your actions and thoughts those of love: at all times, in all things, toward all people. It's the Jesus way of life, and it's the way to life forever with God.

*At Minnesota you get to the game when the game starts. Here, you get here two hours ahead of time so you can see the eagle fly.*
*-- Auburn graduate assistant Tony Levine*

**To live the Jesus way is to act with love at all times,**
**in all things, and toward all people.**

# BLIND JUSTICE

### Read Micah 6:6-8.

*"He has showed you, O man, what is good. And what does the Lord require of you? To act justly and to love mercy and to walk humbly with your God" (v. 8).*

**E**verybody knows Auburn was robbed of a shot at the national championship in 2004, but two decades earlier, the Tigers had the title itself stolen from them.

Auburn faced a brutal schedule in 1983 that included games against seven ranked teams. The schedule suddenly looked even tougher when the Tigers lost to Texas 20-7 in the second game. So all they did after that loss was run the table, going undefeated in the SEC and winning nine straight games that included defeats of Tennessee, Florida State, Florida, Maryland and Boomer Esiason, and Georgia, which had won the last three SEC titles. The win in Athens clinched the SEC championship and a berth in the Sugar Bowl. In the Tiger dressing room after the game, Coach Pat Dye licked sugar off a football.

When Bo Jackson ripped Alabama for 256 yards in a 23-20 win, Auburn was 10-1 and was ranked number three behind Nebraska and Texas.

Al Del Greco's talented toes paced a 9-7 win over No. 8 Michigan in a brutal physical battle in New Orleans on New Year's Day. Then Miami beat Nebraska in the Orange Bowl and Georgia upset Texas in the Cotton Bowl. The Tigers had won the national

championship on the field – or so it seemed until the next day. To the dismay of Auburn fans everywhere, the polls kept Auburn at number three, behind Miami and Nebraska.

Coach Pat Dye was blunt in his assessment of Miami's being voted number one: "I'd say that was as big an injustice as I've seen as far as crowning a national champion."

Where's the justice when cars fly past you just as a state trooper pulls you over? When a con man swindles an elderly neighbor? When crooked politicians treat your tax dollars as their personal slush fund? When children starve?

Injustice enrages us, but anger is not enough. The establishment of justice in this world has to start with each one of us. The Lord requires it of us. For most of us, a just world is one in which everybody gets what he or she deserves.

But that is not God's way. God expects us to be just and merciful in all our dealings without consideration as to whether the other person "deserves" it. The justice we dispense should truly be blind.

If that doesn't sound "fair," then pause and consider that when we stand before God, the last thing we want is what we deserve. We want mercy, not justice.

*None of us wants justice from God. What we want is mercy because if we got justice, we'd all go to hell.*

*-- Bobby Bowden*

**God requires that we dispense justice and mercy
without regards to deserts, exactly what we pray
we will in turn receive from God.**

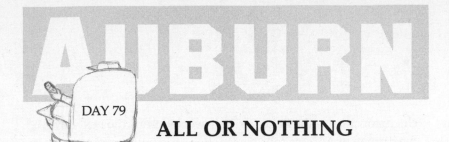

DAY 79

# ALL OR NOTHING

### Read Deuteronomy 6:4-9.

*"Love the Lord your God with all your heart and with all your soul and with all your strength" (v. 5).*

**W**hen a neighbor asked Torrance A. "Bo" Russell's daughter what the "A" stood for, she told him "Auburn." It wasn't true, but it certainly could have been, for Bo Russell was an Auburn man to the core right to the day he died.

Russell wanted to play football for Auburn so badly that he declined scholarship offers from other schools to walk on in 1935. One of Auburn's greatest linemen ever, he was a three-year letterman at tackle; in 1938, he was All-SEC, team captain, and Most Valuable Player. He played two seasons in the NFL and was inducted into the Alabama Sports Hall of Fame in 1979.

He participated in some great adventures at Auburn. He was on the 1936 squad that went to Havana, Cuba, for the Rhumba Bowl. On the boat trip over, he met Jesse Owens, who was on his way to race a horse as part of the sports festival that included Auburn's bowl game. Russell remembered that Owens won.

That same team played Santa Clara in San Francisco, which required a train trip of several days. The team did some sight-seeing in Hollywood before enjoying a rather spectacular treat. "We were among the first people other than construction people to cross the Golden Gate Bridge," Russell recalled. "They gave us a private tour of the bridge before it had even opened."

Russell was never far from the university he loved, though. After he came home following World War II, he vowed to do all he could to help Auburn. He was on the search committee that in 1951 recommended the hiring of Shug Jordan.

"Auburn was just always in [Russell's] heart," said one of his daughters. A grandson remembered that everything Russell did "was around Auburn. . . . He was just all Auburn."

Unlike Bo Russell, all too many sports fans cheer their loudest when their team is winning championships, but they're the first to criticize or turn silent when losses and disappointments come. They're fair-weather fans.

The true Auburn fans stick with the Tigers no matter what, which is exactly the way God commands us to love him. Sure, this mandate is eons old, but the principle it established in our relationship with God has not changed. If anything, it has gained even more immediacy in our materialistic, secular culture that demands we love and worship anything and anybody but God.

Moreover, since God gave the original command, he has sent us Jesus. Thus, we today are even more indebted to God's grace and have even more reason to love God than did the Israelites to whom the original command was given.

God gave us everything; in return, we are to love him with everything we have and everything we are.

*He loved Auburn more than anything, except me.*
*-- Ann Russell, about her husband, Bo*

**With all we have and all we are –**
**that's the way we are to love God.**

# THE INTERVIEW

### Read Romans 14:1-12.

*"We will all stand before God's judgment seat. . . . So then, each of us will give an account of himself to God" (vv. 10, 12).*

**A**uburn assistant football coach Don Dunn once interviewed for a job standing in a bathroom.

Dunn came to Auburn from Ole Miss with Tommy Tuberville in 1999 as an assistant defensive coach. Back in 1983, though, he got his start exactly the way many college coaches do – as a graduate assistant. In *A War in Dixie*, Ivan Maisel and Kelly Whiteside declared that the graduate assistant is "coach, gopher, den mother, attendance taker, and whatever else needs to be done at the moment."

It's a rotten job, but it's also a "rite of passage," a foot in the door of the college coaching profession, and Dunn took it – even though his job interview was more than slightly unorthodox. When Dunn showed up in his new suit and shiny shoes to interview with Johnny Majors at Tennessee, the coach was in the shower. Majors promptly called for Dunn to come on in.

Dunn recalled, "I'm standing at the edge of the shower, the place is filled with steam, and I'm already a nervous wreck. And he's soaping himself and I am talking to him and all he said was, 'Are you ready to be a Volunteer?' And I said, 'Yes, sir.' And he said, 'Go up and see so and so.' And that was my interview."

# TIGERS

When Dunn picked up his wife, he told her, "I'm a volunteer." "That's great," she answered. "I've always loved the Tennessee Volunteers." "No, you don't understand," Dunn said. "I'm a *volunteer.*" The average graduate student works about seventeen hours a day during football season. That grinding job requiring more than one hundred hours a week for which Dunn had interviewed in a bathroom didn't include any paycheck.

You know all about job interviews even if you've never had one in a steam-filled bathroom. You've experienced the stress, the anxiety, the helpless feeling. You tried to appear calm and relaxed, struggling to come up with reasonably original answers to banal questions and to cover up the fact that you thought the interviewer was a total geek. You told yourself that if they turned you down, it was their loss, not yours.

You won't be so indifferent, though, about your last interview: the one with God. A day will come when we will all stand before God to account for ourselves. It is to God and God alone – not our friends, not our parents, not society in general – that we must give a final and complete account.

Since all eternity will be at stake, it sure would help to have a surefire reference with you. One – and only one -- is available: Jesus Christ.

*I hereby apply for the head coaching job at Auburn.*
*-- Shug Jordan's complete job application in 1951*

**You will have one last interview -- with God --**
**and you sure want Jesus there with you**
**as a character witness.**

# THE LEADER

**Read Matthew 16:13-19.**

*"You are Peter, and on this rock I will build my church, and the gates of Hades will not overcome it" (v. 18).*

If ever the Auburn football team of 2004 needed a leader, this was the moment.

The Tigers were 2-0 and ranked 14th after wins over Louisiana-Monroe and Mississippi State, but the fourth-ranked LSU Tigers blew into town as the defending national champions and the favorites. For most of the game, they played the part, leading 9-3 when Auburn got the ball at its 40 with only 6:37 to play. If Auburn was truly going to be a championship contender, somebody had to step forward and lead right now. Somebody did.

That somebody was quarterback Jason Campbell, who had "endured considerable criticism and blame throughout the 2003 season and still had so much to prove – not only to the fans, but to his coaches, teammates and himself." So when Campbell stepped into the huddle with all the pressure of the season on his shoulders, he took charge. Guard Danny Lindsey remembered that Campbell said, "Y'all get me the best protection you can give because we're fixin' to go down and score and win the game." Said Lindsey, "We believed him." "When I heard Jason say that," wide receiver Courtney Taylor said, "I knew it was our time."

It was. Campbell led the Tigers on the legendary 60-yard drive that pulled out a 10-9 win. Tight end Cooper Wallace said, "Jason

definitely showed a lot of leadership right there. He kept talking to us in the huddle, calming us down." The touchdown came when Campbell hit Taylor with a 16-yard pass with only 1:14 left.

Jason Campbell led the Tigers all the way to an undefeated season.

Every aspect of life that involves people – every organization, every group, every project, every team -- must have a leader. If goals are to be reached, somebody must take charge.

The early Christian church was no different. Jesus knew this, so he designated the leader in Simon Peter, who was, in fact, quite an unlikely choice to assume such an awesome, world-changing responsibility. In *Twelve Ordinary Men,* John MacArthur described Simon as "ambivalent, vacillating, impulsive, unsubmissive." Hardly a man to inspire confidence in his leadership skills. Yet, Peter became, according to MacArthur, "the greatest preacher among the apostles" and the "dominant figure" in the birth of the church.

The implication for your own life is obvious and unsettling. You may think you lack the attributes necessary to make a good leader for Christ. But consider Simon Peter, an ordinary man who allowed Christ to rule his life and became the foundation upon which the Christian church was built.

*Leadership, like coaching, is fighting for the hearts and souls of men and getting them to believe in you.*
*-- Legendary Grambling Coach Eddie Robinson*

**God's leaders are men and women**
**who allow Jesus to lead them.**

# FATHERS AND SONS

**Read Matthew 3:13-17.**

*"A voice from heaven said, 'This is my Son, whom I love; with him I am well pleased'" (v. 17).*

**D**ad, this is what we came for."

So thought Joe Beckwith at a moment in his life of crowning achievement: pitching in the 1985 World Series. "I couldn't see my dad," Beckwith said of his moment to cherish, "but I knew where he was."

Growing up, Joe was close to his father, Bill, who was the business manager for the Auburn athletic department. "My dad was in charge of track meets," he recalled. "Whatever was happening, I was there. It was every kid's dream."

Dad's sharp eye shaped the course of Joe's life. Playing Dixie Youth ball as a youngster, Joe was a catcher who pitched occasionally until his father noticed that his son threw the ball back harder than the pitcher threw it to the plate. That observation started Joe on a path that saw him realize dreams most boys can only imagine. He began to practice pitching in his back yard using tree roots as a mound. "I decided my junior year [in high school] I wanted to play baseball," he said.

When college recruiters started showing up, Joe listened only to Auburn coach Paul Nix. To spurn Auburn would have been turning his back on family. Literally.

Joe Beckwith lettered four years at Auburn (1974-77) and set

# TIGERS

a school and SEC record with 31 career wins. He pitched eight seasons in the majors that included appearances in two World Series.

And always, he had that close bond with his father.

American society largely belittles and marginalizes fathers and their influence upon their sons. Men are perceived as necessary to effect pregnancy; after that, they can leave and everybody's better off.

But we need look in only two places to appreciate the enormity of that misconception: our jails – packed with males who lacked the influence of fathers in their lives as they grew up -- and the Bible. God – being God – could have chosen any relationship he desired between Jesus and himself, including society's approach of irrelevancy. Instead, the most important relationship in all of history was that of father-son.

God obviously believes a close, loving relationship between fathers and sons, such as that of Joe and Bill Beckwith, is crucial. For men and women to espouse otherwise or for men to walk blithely and carelessly out of their children's lives constitutes disobedience to the divine will.

Simply put, God loves fathers. After all, he is one.

*My dad was a huge influence on me. I imagine if he had put a wrench in my hand I would have been a great mechanic.*
*-- Pete Maravich*

**Fatherhood is a tough job, but a model**
**for the father-child relationship is found in that**
**of Jesus the Son with God the Father.**

# MUDSLINGING

### Read Isaiah 1:15-20.

*"Though your sins are like scarlet, they shall be as white as snow; though they are red as crimson, they shall be like wool" (v. 18).*

The field was so muddy that Auburn's coach ordered his players into the showers at halftime so he could tell who was who.

In 1942, the Tigers made what Clyde Bolton called in *War Eagle* "a miserable trip" to Washington, D.C., to play Georgetown. The team traveled by train and stopped overnight in Lynchburg, Va., for practice and supper, but the train did not budge during the night because of a flood down the line.

The Tigers thus arrived in D.C. late and found they had no transportation to the field. The players stood on street corners and hailed taxis whenever they happened by.

When they finally made it to the stadium, the team discovered that the field was "a hog wallow." Not only had the Washington Redskins practiced on it after a rainstorm, but a Friday night game completed the conversion to a quagmire and what Bolton called "impossible" playing conditions.

After one play, the muddied players from both teams looked exactly alike. One Georgetown player tried to take advantage of the situation by sneaking into the Tiger huddle. When Auburn complained, a bewildered ref had to ask the Tigers which player was the offender; he sure couldn't tell.

# TIGERS

Even Auburn head coach Jack Meagher couldn't identify his dirty players. At halftime, he ordered his team into the showers, clothes and all, so he could sort them out himself. The miserable game ended in an uninspiring 6-6 tie with the Auburn players and coaches having to ride a flatbed truck back to the hotel.

Maybe you've never slopped any pigs and thus have never traipsed around a "hog wallow." You may not be a fan of mud boggin'. Still, you've worked on your car, planted a garden, played touch football in the rain, or endured some military training. You've been dirty.

Dirt, grime, and mud aren't the only sources of stains, however. We can also get dirty spiritually by not living in accordance with God's commands, by doing what's wrong, or by not doing what's right. We all experience temporary shortcomings and failures; we all slip and fall into the mud.

Whether we stay there or not, though, is a function of our relationship with Jesus. For the followers of Jesus, sin is not a way of life; it's an abnormality, so we don't stay in the filth. We seek a spiritual bath by expressing regret and asking for God's pardon in Jesus' name. God responds by washing our soul white as snow with his forgiveness.

*An athlete's journey towards perfection is often times paved with mud, blood, sweat, and tears.*
*— Paralympic gold medal winner Sarah Will*

**When your soul gets dirty,**
**a powerful and thorough cleansing agent**
**is available for the asking: God's forgiveness.**

# THROUGH THE DOOR

**Read Revelation 3:14-22.**

*"Here I am! I stand at the door and knock. If anyone hears
my voice and opens the door, I will come in" (v. 20).*

In the dark of the night, the screen door creaked – and so yet
another one was gone.

Shug Jordan had a tough task on his hands when he ran his
first spring training in 1951. He had to find out who could play
football and who was just along for the free ride. "We didn't know
anything about our squad except that Auburn had won only three
games in the last three years," Jordan said. "We didn't know the
players, just a few names and that there was enough material to
win more games than they had been winning. It was mysterious,
even eerie."

So Jordan conducted a camp that Buck Bradberry, the defensive
backfield coach, described as "Marine boot camp football. It was
survival of the fittest." Some would-be players didn't even bother
to show up once word got around about how tough the practices
would be. Jordan himself later said, "I don't think we've had
another spring as demanding as the first one. It was grim."

George Atkins, who went on to be a star guard, play pro football,
and coach at Auburn under Jordan, said the coaches wanted to
find out "who would go when they were tired and who wouldn't."
Atkins called that spring training "the toughest thing I have ever
been through in my life. We used to live in those little cabins, six

to eight people inside, didn't have air conditioning, windows open, screen doors. At night you could hear a click and hear the screen door creak – one or two more were gone. You wouldn't believe how they quit and left."

The creak of the screen door – and they were gone, lost to glory, lore, fame, and reward as a Tiger football player. The door was too easy to walk through, and staying in those cabins was too hard.

You're all settled down in your favorite chair; your spouse is somewhere in the house; the kids are doing their homework or twittering. It's calm and quiet.

And then someone knocks on the front door. The dog erupts into a barking frenzy. Your spouse calls, "Can you get that?" You tell the kids to answer the door, whereupon they whine in unison, "I'm busy."

So you abandon your chair. A stranger, a friend, or a Girl Scout with cookies -- it makes no difference. You open the door.

How ironic and heartbreaking it is that so many people who willingly open the doors of their homes when anybody knocks keep the doors of their hearts shut when Jesus knocks. That's what Jesus does; he knocks at the door of your heart like a polite and unassuming guest. He'll step inside only if you invite him, but he's the one visitor above all others you want to let in.

*Opportunity may knock, but you must open the door.*
*-- Wrestling sportswriter and official Bill Welker*

**Jesus won't barge into your heart; he will enter only when you open the door and invite him in.**

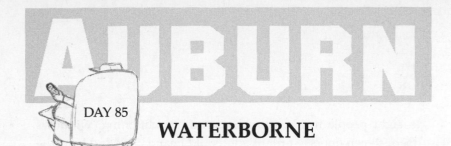

# WATERBORNE

**Read Acts 10:34-48.**

*"Can anyone keep these people from being baptized with water? They have received the Holy Spirit just as we have" (v. 47).*

**T**here's something in the water at Auburn.

Usually it's the swimming and diving teams setting new records and winning more championships. The men's teams: national championships in 2009, 2007, 2006, 2005, 2004, 2003, 1999, and 1997. The women's team: national championships in 2007, 2006, 2004, 2003, and 2002.

From all that recent success, you might think swimming is one of the newer sports at Auburn, but actually it's one of the oldest. Auburn had what was then called a "tank team" back in 1932, five years before swimming was recognized as a sport by the SEC.

Even before the team was officially established, Auburn competed in "telegraphic" meets. The pool, which was in the basement of Alumni Gym, was only 55 feet long and 25 feet wide. In three lanes, the athletes swam three laps for 50 meters. They timed themselves and the results were sent to the competing team via telegraph. No records remain of how Auburn fared in those rather quaint meets.

By 1936, the "Paddlers," as they were then known, had swim trunks and robes and took ten swimmers on the road to meets. Not until 1940, when they finished fifth at the championships, did

the Paddlers show up in any official SEC records.

On into the 1950s and '60s, the swimmers were volunteers from the school's mandatory swim classes. The modern era for the swim team began in the 1970s with the hiring of Eddie Reese as coach and the launching of the women's team in 1974, though the women had no scholarships until 1976.

What is in the water at Auburn today is a dynasty with thirteen national championships through 2010.

Children's wading pools and swimming pools in the backyard. Fishing, boating, skiing, and swimming at a lake. Sun, sand, and surf at the beach. If there's any water around, we'll probably be in it, on it, or near it. If there's not any at hand, we'll build a dam and create our own.

We love the wet stuff for its recreational uses, but water first and foremost is about its absolute necessity to support and maintain life. From its earliest days, the Christian church appropriated water as an image of life through the ritual of baptism. Since the time of the arrival of the Holy Spirit at Pentecost, baptism with water has been the symbol of entry into the Christian community. It is water that marks a person as belonging to Jesus. It is through water that a person proclaims that Jesus is his Lord.

There's something in the water, all right. There is life.

*Swimmers are like teabags; you don't know how strong they are until you put them in the water.*

*– Source unknown*

**There is life in the water:**
**physical life and spiritual life.**

# THE SCAPEGOAT

**Read Leviticus 16:15-22.**

*"He is to lay both hands on the head of the live goat and
confess over it all the wickedness and rebellion of the
Israelites — all their sins — and put them on the goat's
head" (v. 21).*

**B**uilding a new football stadium always means overcoming a
number of obstacles. In Jordan-Hare's case, that included goats.

In the early days, the Tigers played football on the "drill field,"
which is now a park and a parking lot. In the 1920s, the team
moved to Drake Field, which had temporary bleachers erected
every year. Total seating capacity was about 700. With such
limited seating, home games were not a financial windfall, and
Auburn usually played only one home game a year.

Late in the 1930s, the need for a larger stadium was widely
accepted by those close to the program. Former athletic director
Jeff Beard, who as a student helped assemble the temporary
bleachers, said, "There was a terrible need for a stadium . . . if we
were going to compete with the rest of the schools in the Southern
Conference."

As football coach Jack Meagher improved the team and the
schedule, Auburn's success "began to give Auburn people the
feeling that Auburn should have a home stadium to play in." By
1937, the decision had been made to construct a permanent facility.
Beard helped survey the area for Auburn Stadium, driving in the

first stake. The Tigers have played on that site ever since.

Two problems had to be addressed. A stream at the bottom of the valley had to be diverted, and some tenants had to be evicted. A herd of goats that belonged to the dean of the vet school called the valley home and had to be relocated before construction could begin.

A particular type of goat -- a scapegoat – could really be useful. Mess up at work? Bring him in to get chewed out. Make a decision your children don't like? Let him put up with the whining and complaining. Forget your anniversary? Call him in to grovel and explain.

What a set-up! You don't have to pay the price for your mistakes, your shortcomings, and your failures. You get off scot-free. Exactly the way forgiveness works with Jesus.

Our sins separate us from God because we the unholy can't stand in the presence of the holy God. To remove our guilt, God requires a blood sacrifice. Out of his unimaginable love for us, he provided the sacrifice: his own son. Jesus is the sacrifice made for us; through Jesus and Jesus alone, forgiveness and eternity with God are ours.

It's a bumper sticker, but it's true: We aren't perfect; we're just forgiven.

*I never blame myself when I'm not hitting. I just blame the bat, and if it keeps up, I change bats.*

*– Yogi Berra*

**For all those times you fail God, you have Jesus
to take the guilt and the blame for you.**

# HOMEBODIES

### Read 2 Corinthians 5:1-10.

*"We . . . would prefer to be away from the body and at home with the Lord" (v. 8).*

There's no place like home, and for one glorious, record-setting stretch, the Auburn women's basketball team was the ultimate bunch of homebodies.

On Feb. 2, 1986, the Tiger women lost to Kentucky in double overtime on their home court. After that night, they began a march to a remarkable accomplishment. Playing in the toughest women's basketball conference in the country, they did not lose again at home until Nov. 24, 1991, when they fell to Northwestern in the second game of the 1991-92 season.

With such players as Vickie Orr, Carolyn Jones, and Mae Ola and Ruthie Bolton leading the way, the Auburn women set an NCAA record by winning 68 straight home games, breaking the previous mark of 62 held by Louisiana Tech.

Orr's career at Auburn was one of the greatest in SEC history. She was a three-time All-America and SEC Player of the Year in 1988.

Mae Ola Bolton was SEC Freshman of the Year in 1985; Ruthie followed suit in 1986. Ruthie's jersey was retired in 2001. Their coach, Joe Ciampi, said the sisters were "critical in Auburn's drive to national prominence."

Carolyn Jones was a two-time All-American guard in 1990 and

# TIGERS

1991 whose jersey was also retired in 2001. (See devotion No. 65.)

Ciampi was the Tiger head coach during that remarkable run, but he never really talked to his team about the streak, and setting the record was never a goal for the Tigers. Instead, Ciampi remarked that the streak "was just another step on the ladder to help us be successful in our ultimate goal," which was to win a national championship.

Still, nobody in the history of the women's college game to that point had loved playing at home or done a better job of it than had the Auburn Tigers.

Home is not necessarily a matter of geography. It may be that place you share with your spouse and your children, whether it's Alabama or Alaska. You may feel at home when you return to Auburn, wondering why you were so eager to leave in the first place. Maybe the home you grew up in still feels like an old shoe, a little worn but comfortable and inviting.

God planted that sense of home in us because he is a God of place, and our place is with him. Thus, we may live a few blocks away from our parents and grandparents or we may relocate every few years, but we will still sometimes feel as though we don't really belong no matter where we are. We don't; our true home is with God in the place Jesus has gone ahead to prepare for us. We are homebodies and we are perpetually homesick.

*Everybody's better at home.*
*— Basketball player Justin Dentmon*

**We are continually homesick for our real home,
which is with God in Heaven.**

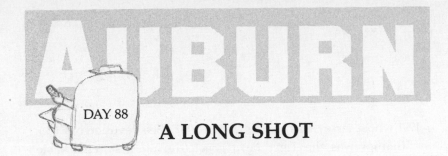

# A LONG SHOT

**Read Matthew 9:9-13.**

*"[Jesus] saw a man named Matthew sitting at the tax collector's booth. 'Follow me,' he told him, and Matthew got up and followed him" (v. 9).*

The quarterback who at the time had the greatest season in Auburn football history was a long shot ever to play college football – or any football at all. He was too sickly as a child.

In 1997, Dameyune Craig had the season of his life. The senior led Auburn to the SEC West title and within two points of the SEC championship. He passed for a school-record 3,277 yards and 18 touchdowns. He was All-SEC and finished with Auburn records for total yards in one game (445 vs. Army), most completions in a season (216), most career 300-yard passing games (six), and most consecutive games with a touchdown pass (13).

All the while, Craig played with a health problem that as a child apparently put him on the sidelines for good and made his dreams of playing quarterback for Auburn a long shot.

As Craig grew up in Mobile, his parents wouldn't allow him to compete in organized sports, but not because they were overprotective. Their son had asthma, which was "so bad my mom used to rush me to the emergency room quite often. It was to the point that I used to get so many shots I became immune to needles."

His asthma condition improved, though, when he entered his teens. Still, he had to talk his parents into letting him go out

for his middle school's football team. "I had a pretty good year," Craig recalled.

The rest is history. Craig's asthma flared up occasionally at Auburn, requiring one of those needles that didn't bother him anymore. It didn't slow him down, though, as the long shot not only played but became part of Auburn lore.

Matthew the tax collector was another long shot, an unlikely person to be a confidant of the Son of God. While we may not get all warm and fuzzy about the IRS, our government's revenue agents are nothing like Matthew and his ilk. He bought a franchise, paying the Roman Empire for the privilege of extorting, bullying, and stealing everything he could from his own people. Tax collectors of the time were "despicable, vile, unprincipled scoundrels."

And yet, Jesus said only two words to this lowlife: "Follow me." Jesus knew that this long shot would make an excellent disciple.

It's the same with us. While we may not be quite as vile as Matthew was, none of us can stand before God with our hands clean and our hearts pure. We are all impossibly long shots to enter God's Heaven. That is, until we do what Matthew did: get up and follow Jesus.

*Nobody really thought I was going to be a good football player because I was so sick all of the time.*

*-- Dameyune Craig on his childhood*

**Only through Jesus does our status change
from being long shots to enter God's Kingdom
to being heavy favorites.**

# FAITHFUL LIVES

**Read Hebrews 11:1-12.**

*"Faith is the substance of things hoped for, the evidence of things not seen" (v. 1 NKJV).*

Coach Terry Bowden called what became one of the most memorable plays in Auburn football history even though he wasn't convinced it would work.

The Tigers of 1993 entered the Alabama game 10-0, but they trailed 14-5 in the third quarter and then lost quarterback Stan White to a knee injury. The improbable dream of the 11-0 season was fading away.

Out trotted Patrick Nix, who once admitted, "Based on my ability, I never should have even played at Auburn. I'm a coach now and I don't know if I would sign myself."

Nix faced fourth and 15 at the Alabama 35. That's when Bowden made the call that "in his heart, he didn't expect it to work." Though Nix had had no time to warm up, Bowden called for him for throw deep. The coach reasoned that the Tigers were too far for a field goal attempt, that if the pass were incomplete, "we still had pretty good field position. If it was intercepted, they'd be at their own 5."

Nix threw deep for wide receiver Frank Sanders, who came back to grab the ball and then dived into the end zone. For Nix, who would become the starter in 1994, the play was "the thrill of a lifetime." "I'm still in awe," he said years later. "It was a fairytale.

It still is."

Stunned and suddenly on their heels, Alabama never recovered. A field goal and a 70-yard sprint by James Bostic later Auburn had a 22-14 win.

And the turnaround came on a play in which the coach had no faith.

Your faith forms the heart and soul of what you are. Faith in people, things, ideologies, and concepts to a large extent determines how you spend your life. You believe in the Auburn Tigers, in your family, in the basic goodness of Americans, in freedom and liberty, and in abiding by the law. These beliefs mold you and make you the person you are.

This is all great stuff, of course, that makes for decent human beings and productive lives. None of it, however, is as important as what you believe about Jesus.

To have faith in Jesus is to believe his message of hope and salvation as recorded in the Bible. True faith in Jesus, however, has an additional component; it must also include a personal commitment to him. In other words, you don't just believe in Jesus; you live for him.

Faith in Jesus does more than shape your life; it determines your eternity.

*To me, religion – faith – is the only real thing in life.*

*-- Bobby Bowden*

**Your belief system is the foundation
upon which you build a life; faith in Jesus
is the foundation for your eternal life.**

# CHEERS

### Read Matthew 21:1-11.

*"The crowds that went ahead of him and those that followed shouted" (v. 9).*

Don't look for Auburn's earliest football cheer to make a comeback anytime soon.

Dr. George Petrie, the father of Auburn football, remembered that great enthusiasm surrounded Auburn's first-ever football game, which was played against Georgia on Feb. 20, 1892, at Piedmont Park in Atlanta.

Both teams made the trip by train and stayed at the same hotel, the Kimball House. *The Atlanta Constitution* reported that the teams and fans gathered in the lobby and "sounded their yells in thundering chorus which at once brought every guest to the balconies all the way up to the sixth floor, to look down inquiringly. Guests trembled with fear lest the top of the grand old Kimball should be blown off with the vocal force."

Georgia got the cheering started. The Auburn contingent responded by creating the first-ever school cheer on the spot, which went "Rah, rah, ree. Rah, rah, ree. Alabama A.M.C."

Dr. Petrie found the cheer lacking, noting "We couldn't get much punch in it. [Georgia's] yell was a war cry. Ours sounded like a mild announcement." The "AMC" stood for Agricultural and Mechanical College, which was Auburn's name back then.

The cheer sounded a whole lot better after the game, which

# TIGERS

Auburn won in the rain and the mud 10-0. Dr. Petrie said many of the fans "acted like crazy youngsters" after the win. In her excitement, one "charming and gentle lady" conked a stranger with her parasol. Exuberant fans grabbed Auburn's center "and before anyone could stop them, hustled him into their buggy, squeezed him in between them, all muddy as he was, and drove [away] shouting: 'Rah, rah ree. Alabama A.M.C.'"

Chances are you go to work every day, do your job well, and then go home to your family. This country couldn't run without you; you're indispensable to the nation's efficiency. Even so, nobody cheers for you or waves pompoms in your face. Your name probably will never elicit a standing ovation when a PA announcer calls it.

It's just as well, since public opinion is notoriously fickle. Consider what happened to Jesus. When he entered Jerusalem, he was the object of raucous cheering and an impromptu parade. The crowd's adulation reached such a frenzy they tore branches off trees and threw their clothes on the ground.

Five days later the crowd shouted again, only this time they screamed for Jesus' execution.

So don't worry too much about not having your personal set of cheering fans. Remember that you do have one personal cheerleader who will never stop pulling for you: God.

*A cheerleader is a dreamer that never gives up.*

*– Source unknown*

**Just like the sports stars, you do have
a personal cheerleader: God.**

# NOTES
### (by Devotion Day Number)

1    Settlers began building a village . . . returned to Georgia: Clyde Bolton, *War Eagle* (Huntsville, AL: The Strode Publishers, 1973), p. 11.

1    on a business trip where . . . loveliest village of the plain.": Bolton, p. 12.

1    In 1857, the Alabama Conference . . . changed to Auburn University.: Bolton, p. 21.

1    While Auburn professor George Petrie . . . Practices began: Bolton, p. 22.

1    the team challenged Georgia. . . . team had been organized,: Bolton, p. 23.

2    "hit town with fire . . ." the first team meeting: Phillip Marshall, *The Auburn Experience* (Auburn: Phillip Marshall, 2004), p. 94.

2    the first spring training under Dye . . . they could survive anything.: Marshall, p. 94.

2    "built a powerhouse . . . willingness to sacrifice.": Marshall, p. 93.

2    "We worked so hard," . . . harder than anybody else.": Marshall, p. 94.

2    We weren't sure of anything . . . to have to work.: Chris Warner, ed., *SEC Sports Quotes* (Baton Rouge: CEW Enterprises, 2002, p. 81.

3    She lettered four years . . . LaKeisha Johnson the outside hitter: Beth Farnsworth, "Former Basketball Player Succeeds in Volleyball," *The Auburn Plainsman*, Sept. 11, 2003, http://www.theplainsman.com/vews/display.v/ART/2003/09/11, Aug. 29, 2006.

4    Some 42,000 soaked fans shivered under raincoats and umbrellas,: Wayne Hester, *Where Tradition Began* (Birmingham: Seacoast Publishing/*The Birmingham News*, 1991), p. 58.

4    "a ground-skinner pitchout": Hester, p. 58.

4    "was cold and clammy . . . Great day, wonderful day.": Hester, p. 59.

4    "never had such a celebration broke[n] out on an Auburn sideline.": Hester, p. 59.

4    Nobody knows how hard . . . They're going to win it.: Hester, p. 59.

5      The noise was so intense . . . Jesse going the other way,":
Hester, p. 181.

6      Kolen has said that he . . . wife my sophomore year.": Carten
Cordell, "Glory Days," *The Auburn Plainsman*, Sept. 2,
2004, http://www.theplainsman.com/vnews/display.v/
ART/2004/09/02, Aug. 28, 2006.

7      Head coach Chris Fox said . . . in a long time.": Brittany Griffith, "Rain Doesn't Slow Cross Country Teams at Home Meet,"
*The Auburn Plainsman*, Oct. 16, 2003, http://www.theplainsman.
com/vnews/display.v/ART/2003/10/16, Aug. 30, 2006.

7      It was fun," . . . their favorite athletes home.: Griffith.

7      It takes a special . . . here in the rain.: Griffith.

8      "a man before his time" . . . back in the Southeastern Conference.": Marshall, p. 96.

8      "I was a kid that . . . to recruit all along.": Marshall, p. 96.

8      "I figured they'd tell me to go home right then,": Marshall,
p. 96.

9      "the third wheel in the Bowl Championship Series": John
Zenor, "Auburn Perfect, But Frustrated," Jan. 6, 2005, http://
www.amarillo.com/stories/010605/col_972252.shtml, Dec. 20,
2008.

9      "I was disappointed that . . . "I beg to differ.": Zenor.

9      "You can't do any better.": Zenor.

10     "They" were several hundred . . . to welcome him.: Bolton,
p. 74.

10     When the train pulled into . . . stared at each other.": Bolton,
p. 74.

10     "the most disgusted bunch . . . gotten a Mickey Rooney.:
Bolton, p. 74.

10     "steaming, black train": Bolton, p. 74.

11     When she was 15 and . . . able to do what I want.": Linda
Hallmark, "Auburn U. Student Competes on Higher Level,"
http://www.cstv.com/sports/w-golf/uwire/022405aad.html,
Dec. 20, 2008.

12     What Bowden saw at Auburn . . . pins that emphasized
their Attitude.": Carten Cordell, "Five Years Later, Terry
Talks," *The Auburn Plainsman*, April 8, 2004, http://www.the
plainsman.com/vnews/display.v/ART/2004/04/08, Sept. 1, 2006.

12     We just tried to create a positive attitude.: Cordell, "Five
Years Later."

13     "I didn't weight but 146, . . . you finished it.":

# AUBURN

Bolton, p. 139.

13    when Auburn played Army . . . liked to have gotten out.":
      Bolton, p. 139.

13    As the score mounted, . . . cussingest quarterback I ever saw.":
      Bolton, p. 140.

13    Don't cuss. . . . And don't lose the game.: Warner, p. 77.

14    "I have worked hard , . . to see your family and friends,": Yi,
      Yun Mi, "Center Gives Opponents Payne," *The Auburn Plains-
      man*, Jan. 27, 2005, http://www.cstv.com/sports/w-baskbl/
      uwire/012705/abn.html, Dec. 21, 2008.

15    No soap or hot water. No pork or pastry.: Bolton, p. 68.

15    "prolate spheroid – that is, . . . to fumble this football.: Bolton,
      p. 65.

15    credited with bringing . . . the hidden ball trick.: Bolton, p. 68.

15    "should be masterful and commanding, even dictatorial.":
      Bolton, p. 67.

15    At times he must be . . . little short of czar.": Bolton, p. 68.

15    no two end runs should . . . 30 yards of your own goal.: Bolton,
      p. 69.

15    His teams were to punt . . . with your head up.": Bolton, p. 70.

16    the first and only Rhumba Bowl.: Bolton, p. 168.

16    The Cuban excursion into football . . . and by boat to Cuba,:
      Bolton, p. 169.

16    most of the players had never been on a boat before.: Bolton,
      p. 170.

16    Trainer Wilbur Hutell loaded a bunch . . . were good for sea-
      sickness.: Bolton, pp. 169-70.

16    five of the players, . . . was sick as a dog.": Bolton, p. 170.

16    The Cubans knew little . . . cared even less.: Bolton, p. 169.

16    Despite predictions of a sellout, fewer than 9,000 folks showed
      up.: Bolton, p. 171.

16    The crowd got really excited . . . when it was snapped,":
      Bolton, p. 172.

17    the sixth-ranked Miami Hurricanes . . . second Miami extra
      point try,: Hester, p. 47.

17    He pulled some of his starters off the field to talk to them.:
      Hester, p. 47.

17    Jordan told his team . . . Auburn's All-American end Jim
      Pyburn.: Hester, p. 47.

17    "No fullback in the long history . . . football game like
      Childress did.": Hester, p. 47.

**184**

18    "As the final seconds melted. . . the party on the floor.":
      Marshall, p. 169.

18    Coach Cliff Ellis personally saluted . . . the Cliff Dwellers.: Jack
      McCallum, "Flat Out Good," *Sports Illustrated*, March 1, 1999.
      http://vault.sportsillustrated.cnn.com/vault/article/magazine/
      MAG1015189/index.htm, Feb. 26, 2009.

18    "The song 'We Are the Champions' . . . slapped hands all the
      way.: Marshall, p. 169.

18    It was like a . . . The stars came out.": Marshall, p. 169.

18    Bo Jackson flew in from Chicago . . . to press the flesh.:
      McCallum.

18    "What better way to go out . . . you win the SEC champion-
      ship.: Marshall, p. 169.

18    Ellis called the best leader he had ever seen.: Marshall, p. 168.

18    I don't think there's . . . happier than I am.: Marshall, p. 169.

19    "If you had walked down . . . It was a day for history.": Hester,
      p. 137.

19    "Today, for the first time, . . . and Auburn football programs.:
      Hester, p. 194.

19    "It was probably . . . in Auburn football history.": Hester,
      p. 196.

19    Alabama's "coming to Auburn . . . since I've been here.":
      Hester, p. 137.

19    After years of bondage, . . . the Promised Land.: Warner, p. 82.

20    "If you were to write . . . would laugh at it.": Charles Goldberg,
      "Unlikely Hero Pulled Off a 'Miracle' in '02," *The Birmingham
      News*, Nov. 21, 2003, http://nl.newsbank.com/nl-search/we/
      Archives?p_action=doc&p_docid=OFF1FD8B59D, Dec. 25,
      2008.

20    "A miracle" . . . rest of the running backs,": Goldberg.

21    "We didn't have a nickel,": Hester, p. 41.

21    Auburn's athletic department was $100,000 . . . seats on the
      grass.: Hester, p. 41.

21    "That was the turning point," . . . $250,000 in the black.:
      Hester, p. 42.

22    "It was very different," . . . I played too early.": Marshall,
      p. 200.

23    The Battle of Chattahoochee.: Alf Van Hoose quoted by Rich
      Donnell, *Shug* (Montgomery: Owl Bay Publishers, 1993),
      p. 133.

23    Auburn led 14-0 on the way . . . and the benches

emptied.: Donnell, p. 132.

23    "I can still see . . . the boys coming out.": Donnell, pp. 132-33.

23    "fights broke out all over . . . a football player, not a fighter,": Donnell, p. 133.

24    In April 2003 the Florida Gators . . . "what do you expect, coach?": Kara Koscelski, "Lacrosse Goes 1-2 at Home," *The Auburn Plainsman*, April 10, 2003, http://www.theplainsman. com/news/display.v/ART/2003/04/10, Sept. 24, 2006.

25    Coach Shug Jordan took advantage . . . pride in Jordan-Hare Stadium.": Hester, p. 112.

25    annihilated, devastated, . . . known to Tigers.": Hester, p. 114.

25    At the end of the game, . . . have you in Auburn.": Hester, p. 115.

26    three games into the 1999 season: Marshall, p. 215.

26    "It started kind of slowly," . . . to be an Auburn Tiger.": Marshall, p. 216.

26    I know when I wake up . . . ordered by the Lord.: Marshall, p. 216.

27    whose primary responsibility was . . . regardless of who you are.": Ivan Maisel and Kelly Whiteside, *A War in Dixie* (New York: HarperCollins Publishers, 2001, p. 156.

28    in 1892, when two glorious . . . the University of Alabama.: Bolton, p. 40.

28    "presented a handsome appearance . . . young ladies with them.": Bolton, p. 42.

28    The paper detailed the security . . . without sustaining any injury.": Bolton, p. 43.

28    The paper produced . . . or who did what.: Bolton, p. 44.

29    Moore arrived in Alabama . . . "I liked their colors better.": Marshall, p. 281.

29    had scholarship offers from both.: Marshall, p. 281.

29    because her brother had played . . . to be just like him,": Marshall, p. 281.

30    "courtly Southern gentleman.": Hester, p. 35.

30    "Shug's saddest times . . . somebody had gotten hurt.": Hester, p. 37.

30    "If they don't think . . . plantation owner working slaves.": Hester, p. 35.

30    Coach Shug Jordan was . . . he had to do.: Warner, p. 61.

31    "Growing up, I was always . . . "the Eva Goulbourne show.": Marshall, p. 245.

31 more than a foot longer . . . by more than six inches.: Marshall, p. 245.

31 "I was very surprised," . . . would win the national championship.": Marshall, p. 245.

31 You can't even jump . . . Big Mac on it.: Warner, p. 63.

32 the Tigers were heavy underdogs . . . three to five touchdowns.": Bolton, p. 125.

32 "turned the old town . . . Ye Gods!": Bolton, p. 125.

33 the bunch Coach Shug . . . his favorite teams.: Hester, pp. 103-04.

33 "The biggest change in . . . the demise of Auburn.": Hester, p. 103.

33 It's amazing. Some of the greatest . . . true to be a Christian man.: Jim & Julie S. Bettinger,
The Book of Bowden (Nashville: TowleHouse Publishing, 2001), p. 121.

34 As Stacy Danley lay . . . cared for his players.: Marshall, p. 45.

34 "He hated for guys . . . turning point of the game.": Marshall, p. 45.

35 "When you do something special . . . town and university celebrate.": Shea Miller, "1999 Men's NCAA Champions," 2006-07 Auburn Swimming & Diving Media Guide, p. 93. http://grfx.cstv.com/photos/schools/aub/sports/c-swim/auto_pdf/07-guide-4.pdf, Dec. 26, 2008.

35 the Tigers were up against 39 teams and 250 athletes: Miller.

35 "This is a dream come true," . . . The celebration began right there . . . to the coliseum.: Miller.

36 Unhelmeted players let their hair . . . took off downfield.: Bolton, p. 45.

36 Spectators rushed onto the field . . . shaped like a watermelon.: Bolton, p. 49.

36 Referees were anyone from . . . simply to watch a game.: Bolton, p. 45.

36 "unorganized and mischievous,": Bolton, p. 45.

36 A missed season because nobody . . . rather than a level one.: Bolton, p. 50.

36 A player hiding the ball under a jersey. No scoreboard: Bolton, p. 69.

36 A player kicking a field goal . . . ball on his helmet.: Bolton, p. 78.

36 No set time for the first . . . depending upon the

weather.: Bolton, p. 80.

36    Teammates dragging a tackled ball carrier forward.: Bolton, p. 81.

36    handles were sewn . . . easier to toss.: Bolton, p. 81.

37    "We went for the field goal . . . to be mighty important.": Hester, p. 108.

37    "I didn't know what . . . thrill I've ever had.": Hester, p. 108.

38    he had to shout . . . front of the Kentucky bench.: Marshall, p. 181.

38    the Auburn students stormed . . . good enough to play there.": Marshall, p. 181.

38    Pressure is for tires.: Warner, p. 65.

39    "When you're growing up . . . I wanted to go.": Bolton, p. 267.

39    "It felt right being around Coach Jordan," Donnell, p. 217.

39    "He never made outlandish . . . every opportunity to play.: Donnell, p. 216.

39    "I was real excited . . . stood up and cheered.: Bolton, p. 267.

40    the week before the Alabama game . . . any thoughts of quitting.: Hester, p. 163.

40    nobody scored on the first-team defense all season.: Marshall, p. 20.

40    he just wanted to play.: Marshall, p. 139.

41    never lost a game at Auburn as a starting quarterback: Marshall, p. 20.

41    pitched the ball behind halfback . . . and recovered the fumble.": Marshall, p. 21.

42    What White wore was . . . his little friend's gift.: Marshall, p. 150.

42    I don't believe in a . . . you block and tackle.: Warner, p. 85.

43    All nineteen athletes on the NCAA roster contributed points to the win.: Justin Caron, "2003 Men's NCAA Champions," *Auburn Swimming & Diving: 2007-08 Media Guide*, p. 84, http://grfx.cstv.com/photos/schools/aub/sports/c-swim/auto_pdf/0708-SD-MG-4.pdf.

43    "The fact that all 19 . . . I am just delighted.": Caron.

45    "I'd go in [a] restaurant . . . back to his family.": Marshall, p. 183.

45    He grew up in Boligee . . . as a lunchroom helper. Marshall, p, 183.

45    Most folks assumed he . . . such a likeable guy." Marshall, p. 183.

45      Harris was cut . . . a game in the pros.: Marshall, p. 183.

46      Daniel Gibson, who played with Newell, . . . block him to the right.": Bolton, p. 111.

46      During World War I . . . that terrible hole in it.": Bolton, p. 111.

47      "the toughest guy who ever walked.": Bolton, p. 266.

47      "probably the finest example . . . he had about 15 stitches.": Bolton, p. 267.

48      "but his wrestlers loved him . . . competing and lessons in living.: Marshall, p. 298.

48      "Without a doubt, he . . . trusted him with my life.": Marshall, p. 298.

49      who was in the lineup only . . . sitting in stunned silence.: Marshall, p. 209.

50      The scoreboard appeared to show . . . Woodall made his field goal.: Donnell, p. 184.

51      after Feb. 7, 2003, every time . . . he pointed up.: Austin Phillips, "Davis Shoots for NBA," *The Auburn Plainsman*, June 3, 2004, p. B5.

51      "I do that to . . . and be sad,": Phillips, p. B5.

51      "He was more positive . . . in a better place,": Phillips, p. B5.

52      "I wanted to see a guy's eyes and see what's in him," Doug Segrest, "Right Place, Right Time," *The Birmingham News*, Sept. 20, 2009, p. 6B.

52      "a nightmare" for the defense . . . "I knew it was coming," Segrest.

52      "It happened so fast, I didn't believe it at first,": Segrest.

53      Even as they practiced, . . . what their futures held.": Marshall, p. 165.

53      "Not even Auburn players . . . what was going on,": Marshall, p. 165.

54      Henley "was a trash talker . . . send him back to plowing.": Marshall, p. 107.

54      "We took 'em like . . . harder than they did.": Marshall, p. 107.

54      Offensive lineman Mac Lorendo said . . . kill him -- them and us.": Marshall, p. 107.

55      Prior to the 2003 season, . . . of Camden Yard proportions.": "Plainsman Park," *Auburn Baseball: 2008 Media Guide*, p. 2, http://auburntigers.cstv.com/sports/m-basebl-spec-rel/08-aub-m-basebl-guide.html, Jan. 4, 2009.

55      includes its own versions . . . Boston's Fenway Park, "Plainsman Park," p. 4.

55 Front-row box seats . . . 60 feet from home plate. "Plainsman Park," p. 4.

56 I don't think a man ever gets over football.": Bolton, p. 99.

56 He spoke those wistful words when he was 84,: Bolton, p. 95.

56 "sandy and rocky, . . . either cotton or wool.: Bolton, p. 96.

56 "As I remember, most of us . . . sold athletic supplies and suits.: Bolton, p. 98.

56 the alums rode with them. . . . made players out of them.": Bolton, p. 98.

56 "there were one or two cars . . . the train go by,: Bolton, p. 98.

56 the War Eagle battle cry had not yet appeared.: Bolton, p. 99.

56 Auburn is a tradition in my family.: Bolton, p. 95.

57 Five years before the passage . . . putting together a team.: Marshall, p. 275.

57 The players who made . . . only their uniforms and warmups.: Marshall, p. 275.

57 We were happy with anything we got.: Marshall, p. 275.

58 nine years of "humility, . . . across the state could gloat.": Hester, p. 148.

58 Alabama rolled up 23 . . . outgaining the Tigers 445-132,: Hester, p. 148.

58 "Everybody realized it was still within our reach,": Hester, p. 149.

58 "I felt, 'Oh, no. This can't happen,'": Hester, p. 149.

59 What happened in the . . . and LSU infamy.": Marshall, p. 47.

59 "If they run the ball right then, the game is over.": Carten Cordell, "Hall Speaks about LSU Ten Years Later," *The Auburn Plainsman*, Sept. 16, 2004, http://www.theplainsman.com/vnews/display.v/ART/2004/09/16, Aug. 30, 2006.

59 "in their minds, . . . one more chance.'": Cordell, "Hall Speaks about LSU."

59 thrusting one finger into the air . . . game he was ever a part of,: Marshall, p. 47.

60 One Georgia lineman in 1916 . . . and a dozen biscuits.": Bolton, p. 77.

60 "made on a grossly erroneous decision of the umpire.": Bolton, p. 63.

60 "the team was rushed right . . . to rob us of the game.": Bolton, p. 63.

61 Binder is from a tight-knit . . . makes Auburn pretty special.": Robin Martin, "Tiger Profile: Adrienne Binder," Jan. 18, 2007,

http://aubunrigers.cstv.com/sports/c-swim/spec-rel/011807aae.
html, Jan. 4, 2009.

61    Sometimes you have to play with a little pain.: Justin A. Rice,
"Spiller Delivers Knockout Blow," *The State*, Nov. 2, 2008,
http://docs.newsbank.com/s/InfoWeb/aggdocs/News
Bank/12434A3FE4C4F2D8, May 6, 2009.

62    At the 9 a.m. staff meeting . . . staff during the season.: Maisel
and Whiteside, p. 97.

62    The key, he said, was to let . . . got all the talent and ability,":
Maisel and Whiteside, p. 97.

62    "Preparation is key," . . . end of the world either,": Maisel and
Whiteside, p. 97.

63    the most points scored on Alabama since 1907.: Bolton, p. 257.

63    Sullivan's brief life . . . didn't make the first down.: Hester,
p. 36.

63    "Coach Jordan met me as I . . . until the game was over.":
Hester, p. 36

64    They were all played in . . . big teams on wet fields.": Bolton,
p. 182.

64    Shug Jordan had scouted . . . was going to pass or run.":
Bolton, p. 182.

65    Nah, she's a glamour girl.": Marshall, p. 198.

65    Young was an administrative . . . They married in 1998.:
Marshall, p. 198.

66    A native of Ottawa, . . . come and experience it.": Marshall,
p. 264.

67    This was the first season . . . Tech boys appeared nervous.":
Bolton, p. 45.

67    Coach Mike Donahue's younger . . . scored four touchdowns;:
Bolton, p. 120.

67    Ed Shirling scored five touchdown;: Bolton, p. 127.

67    the Auburn players thought . . . ever played against one;:
Bolton, p. 127.

68    At the Battle of the Wilderness . . . for the sake of an Auburn
win.: Jim Phillips, "The Fable of War Eagle," *Auburn Football:
2008 Media Guide*, p. 27, http://auburntigers.cstv.com/sports/m-
footbl/spec-rel/08-fb-media-guide.html, Jan. 5, 2009.

68    There's a closeness . . . the war eagle spirit.: Warner, p. 76.

69    Coach Tommy Tuberville spoke of what . . . and the bad
times.": Damon Lawrence, "Auburn Meets
Michigan in Citrus Bowl," *Columbus Ledger-*

*Enquirer*, Dec. 31, 2000, http://www.accessmylibrary.com/coms2/summary_0286-7238783_ITM?, Jan. 5, 2009.

69     "We wish we had . . . as an Auburn Tiger.": Lawrence.

70     Auburn captain John Shirey, . . . forces of the United States.": Bolton, p. 128.

70     before the largest crowd in the history of Southern intercollegiate football.: Bolton, p. 129.

70     Tech's star was Red Barron, . . . we never hit his face.": Bolton, p. 129.

71     The Auburn band had its origins . . . to celebrate the Allied victory.: "History," *The Auburn University Bands*, http://www.auburn.ed/auband/history, Jan. 6. 2009.

71     Short on fullbacks, . . . ran three times and scored: Bolton, p. 111.

71     occurred in 1946 with the . . . playing instruments in 1950.: "History."

72     "Those memories mean more . . . and winning gold medals.": Ryan Robertson, "Rowdy Gaines Shows He Never Gives Up," *The Auburn Plainsman*, June 27, 2007, http://www.theplainsman.com/node/2711, Jan. 6, 2009.

72     "The pinnacle of success . . . once every four years.": Robertson.

72     that's when conventiohal wisdom . . . competitive swimming standards: Robertson.

72     "It was a long, long . . . was really worth it.": Marshall, p. 241.

73     The presidents of the student bodies . . . and buried it.": Bolton, p. 185.

73     a game was scheduled for 1908 . . . The series simply lapsed.: Bolton, p. 90.

73     Walker Reynolds, an All-Southern . . . Auburn a million dollars.": Bolton, p. 98.

73     Former Auburn Coach Mike Donahue . . . and resume the series,: Bolton, p. 89.

73     Life is short, . . . pay any attention anyway.: Warner, p. 83.

74     the "fumblerooskie" is "a play . . . to pick the ball up.": Hester, p. 202.

74     When you run trick plays . . . folks question your sanity.: Bettinger, p. 32.

75     When they saw the Florida defense, . . . We're going to win.'": Marshall, p. 46.

75     Surrounded by blitzing Gators, . . . was going to catch the

|    | ball.": Marshall, pp. 46-47. |
| 76 | called both improbable and impossible: Marshall, p. 226. |
| 76 | "Who am I to believe . . . only see blessings in my life." Marshall, p. 226. |
| 76 | "It could happen," . . . after such a dreadful start.: Marshall, p. 226. |
| 76 | People think only the . . . much more special than this.: Marshall, p. 226. |
| 77 | "This whole year has been unlike . . . They really couldn't picture that.": Maisel and Whiteside, p. 157. |
| 77 | At Minnesota you get to . . . can see the eagle fly.: Maisel and Whiteside, p. 157. |
| 78 | In the Tiger dressing room . . . sugar off a football.: Marshall, p. 26. |
| 78 | "I'd say that was . . . crowning a national champion.": Marshall, p. 27. |
| 78 | None of us wants justice . . . we'd all go to hell.: Bettinger, p. 69. |
| 79 | When a neighbor asked . . . she told him 'Auburn.': Marshall, p. 135. |
| 79 | Russell wanted to play football . . . to walk on in 1935.: Marshall, p. 135. |
| 79 | On the boat trip over, . . . remembered that Owens won.: Bolton, p. 170. |
| 79 | The team did some sightseeing . . . before it had even opened.": Bolton, 175. |
| 79 | he vowed to do all . . . He was just all Auburn.": Marshall, p. 135. |
| 79 | He loved Auburn more than anything, except me.: Marshall, p. 135. |
| 80 | "coach, gopher, den mother . . . done at the moment.": Maisel and Whiteside, p. 155. |
| 80 | a "rite of passage,": Maisel and Whiteside, p. 155. |
| 80 | When Dunn showed up in his . . . didn't include any paycheck.: Maisel and Whiteside, p. 155. |
| 81 | "endured considerable criticism . . . to his coaches, teammates and himself.": Richard Scott, *An Inside Look at a Perfect Season* (Champaign, IL: Sports Publishing L.L.C., 2005), p. 36. |
| 81 | "Y'all get me the best . . . "We believed him.": Scott, p. 36. |
| 81 | "When I heard Jason . . . it was our time.": Scott, p. 45. |
| 81 | "Jason definitely showed a lot . . . calming us down.": Scott, p. 37. |

81      "ambivalent, vacillating, impulsive,unsubmissive.": John
        MacArthur, *Twelve Ordinary Men* (Nashville: W Publishing
        Group, 2002), p. 39.

81      "the greatest preacher among . . . in the birth of the church.:
        MacArthur, p. 39.

82      Dad, this is what we came for.": Marshall, p. 214.

82      "I couldn't see my dad," . . . "but I knew where he was.":
        Marshall, p. 214.

82      "My dad was in charge . . . It was every kid's dream.":
        Marshall, p. 213.

82      Playing Dixie Youth ball . . . turning his back on family.:
        Marshall, p. 213.

83      "a miserable trip" . . . no transportation to the field.: Bolton,
        p. 179.

83      The players stood on street . . . whenever they happened by.:
        Bolton, pp. 179, 182.

83      "a hog wallow." . . . flatbed trucks back to the hotel.: Bolton,
        p. 182.

84      He had to find out . . . along for the free ride.: Donnell, p. 106.

84      "We didn't know anything about . . . in the last three years."
        Donnell, pp. 105-6.

84       "We didn't know the players, . . . tough the practices would
        be.: Donnell, p. 106.

84      "I don't think we've had . . . It was grim.": Donnell, p. 105.

84      "who would go when they . . . how they quit and left.:
        Donnell, p. 108.

85      Auburn had what was then . . . no scholarships until 1976.:
        "History of Auburn Swimming and Diving," *Auburn Swim-
        ming & Diving 2007-08 Media Guide*, p. 66, http://auburntigers.
        cstv.com/sports/c-swim/spec-rel/aub-07-08-swim-guide.html,
        Jan. 28, 2009.

86      In the early days, the Tigers played . . . relocated before
        construction could begin.: Van Plexico, "The History of
        Jordan-Hare Stadium," http://www.plexico.net/sg/jordanhare/
        jh_history1.html, Jan. 28, 2009.

87      the sisters were "critical in Auburn's drive to national
        prominence.": Marshall, p. 197.

87      he never really talked to his . . . successful in our ultimate
        goal,": Paul Newberry, "Home Bodies," *The Birmingham News*,
        Jan. 31, 1991, p. 5F.

88      As Craig grew up in Mobile, . . . I had a pretty good year,":
**194**

Mark Murphy, *Game of My Life: Auburn* (Champaign, IL: Sports Publishing L.L.C., 2007), p. 39.

88    Craig's asthma flared up . . . requiring one of those needles: Murphy, p. 40.

88    "despicable, vile, unprincipled scoundrels.": MacArthur, p. 152.

88    Nobody really thought I was . . . so sick all of the time.: Murphy, p. 39.

89    "Based on my ability, . . . if I would sign myself.": Marshall, p. 30.

89    "in his heart, he didn't expect . . . be at their own 5.": Marshall, p. 30.

89    "the thrill of a lifetime." . . . It still is.": Marshall, p. 29.

89    To me, religion – faith – is the only real thing in life.: Bettinger, p. 44.

90    Both teams made the trip . . . blown off with the vocal force.": Bolton, p. 31.

90    Georgia got the cheering started. . . . like a mild announcement.: Bolton, p. 34.

90    many of the fans acted . . . Alabama A.M.C.": Bolton, p. 35.

# BIBLIOGRAPHY

Bettinger, Jim & Julie S. *The Book of Bowden*. Nashville: TowleHouse Publishing, 2001.

Bolton, Clyde. *War Eagle: A Story of Auburn Football*. Huntsville, AL: The Strode Publishers, 1973.

Caron, Justin. "2003 Men's NCAA Champions." *Auburn Swimming & Diving: 2007-08 Media Guide*. 84. http://grfx.cstv.com/photos/schools/aub/sports/c-swim/auto_pdf/0708-SD-MG-4.pdf.

Cordell, Carten. "Five Years Later, Terry Talks." *The Auburn Plainsman*. 8 April 2004. http://www.theplainsman.com/vnews/display.v/ART/2004/04/08.

---. "Glory Days." *The Auburn Plainsman*. 2 Sept. 2004. http://www.theplainsman.com/vnews/display.v/ART/2004/09/02.

---. "Hall Speaks about LSU Ten Years Later." *The Auburn Plainsman*, 16 Sept. 2004. http://www.theplainsman.com/vnews/display.v/ART/2004/09/16.

Culpepper, R. Alan. "The Gospel of Luke: Introduction, Commentary, and Reflections." *The New Interpreter's Bible*. Vol. IX (Nashville: Abingdon Press, 1998). 1-490.

Donnell, Rich. *Shug: The Life and Times of Auburn's Ralph 'Shug Jordan*. Montgomery: Owl Bay Publishers, 1993.

Farnsworth, Beth. "Former Basketball Player Succeeds in Volleyball. *The Auburn Plainsman*. 11 Sept. 2003. http://www.theplainsman.com/
vnews/display.v/ART/2003/09/11.

Goldberg, Charles. "Unlikely Hero Pulled Off a 'Miracle' in '02." *The Birmingham News*. 21 Nov. 2003. http://nl.newsbank.con/nl-search/we/Archives
?p_action=doc&p_docid=OFF1FD8B59D.

Griffith, Brittany. "Rain Doesn't Slow Cross Country Teams at Home Meet." *The
Auburn Plainsman*. 16 Oct. 2003. http://www.theplainsman.com/vnews/
display.v/ART/2003/10/16.

Hallmark, Linda. "Auburn U. Student Competes on Higher Level." http://www.
cstv.com/sports/w-golf/uwire/022405aad.html.

Hester, Wayne. *Where Tradition Began: The Centennial History of Auburn Football*.
Birmingham: Seacoast Publishing/*The Birmingham News*, 1991.

"History." *The Auburn University Bands*. http://www.auburn.edu/auband/
history.

"History of Auburn Swimming and Diving." *Auburn Swimming &
Diving 2007-08 Media Guide*. 66-67. http://auburntigers.cstv.com/sports/c-
swim/spec-rel/aub-07-08-swim-guide.html.

Koscelski, Kara. "Lacrosse Goes 1-2 at Home." *The Auburn Plainsman*. 10 April
2003. http://www.theplainsman.com/news/display.v/ART/2003/04/10.

Lawrence, Damon. "Auburn Meets Michigan in Citrus Bowl." *Columbus Ledger-
Enquirer*. 31 Dec. 2000. http://www.accessmylibrary.com/coms2/
summary_0286-7238783_ITM?.

MacArthur, John. *Twelve Ordinary Men*. Nashville: W Publishing Group, 2002.

Maisel, Ivan and Kelly Whiteside. *A War in Dixie*. New York: HarperCollins
Publishers, 2001.

Marshall, Phillip. *The Auburn Experience: The Traditions and Heroes of Auburn
Athletics*. Auburn: Phillip Marshall, 2004.

Martin, Robin. "Tiger Profile: Adrienne Binder." 18 Jan. 2007. http://auburn
tigers.cstv.com/sports/c-swim/spec-rel/011807aae.html.

McCallum, Jack. "Flat Out Good." *Sports Illustrated*. 1 March 1999. http://vault.
sportsillustrated.cnn.com/vault/article/magazine/MAG1015189/index.htm.

Miller, Shea. "1999 Men's NCAA Champions." *2006-07 Auburn Swimming &
Diving Media Guide*. 93. http://grfx.cstv.com/photos/schools/aub/sports/c-
swim/auto_pdf/07-guide-4.pdf.

Murphy, Mark. *Game of My Life: Auburn: Memorable Stories of Tigers Football*.
Champaign, IL: Sports Publishing L.L.C., 2007.

Newberry, Paul. "Home Bodies: NCAA Record of 63 Consecutive Home Victories Within Reach of Lady Tigers." *The Birmingham News*. 31 Jan. 1991. 5F.

Phillips, Austin. "Davis Shoots for NBA." *The Auburn Plainsman*. 3 June 2004. B5,
B6.

Phillips, Jim. "The Fable of War Eagle." *Auburn Football: 2008 Media Guide*. 27.
http://auburntigers.cstv.com/sports/m-footbl/spc-rel/08-fb-medi-aguide.
html.

"Plainsman Park." *Auburn Baseball: 2008 Media Guide*. 2, 4. http://auburntigers.
cstv.com/sports/m-basebl/spec-rel/08-aub-m-basebl-guide.html.